GLYPH

GLYPH

Vol. 30

Editorial Staff

BRANDON BROWN, MADELEINE SARDINA, KYLIE YOCKEY

Editor in Chief

BRIANNA NEUMANN

Graphic Design

LEXI MALONE & MADELEINE SARDINA

Santa Fe University Press
Santa Fe University of Art and Design
1600 Saint Michael's Drive
Santa Fe, NM 87505

Printed in the United States
Published by Santa Fe University Press, New Mexico, USA

ISBN: 978-1-387-73129-9

THE LITERARY MAGAZINE OF SANTA FE UNIVERSITY OF ART AND DESIGN IS A COLLECTION OF CREATIVE WORKS BY SFUAD STUDENTS. IT IS A PUBLICATION OF THE CWL DEPARTMENT OFFERED IN SUPPORT OF THE CREATIVE WRITING MAJOR.

THE PIECES IN THIS JOURNAL WERE SELECTED BY THE EDITORS IN A BLIND VOTE. EDITORS WERE NOT PERMITTED TO VOTE ON THEIR OWN PIECES.

GLYPH

THE LITERARY MAGAZINE OF
SANTA FE UNIVERSITY OF ART & DESIGN

CONTENTS

A Letter From the Editors

Dear readers,

We are really incredibly proud to present the 30th edition of Glyph to you. It couldn't have happened without so many people and so much hard work, but it especially couldn't have happened without eyes like yours to read it. So our first thank you is to you – thank you, for picking this book up and for believing in us.

We also need to say a very loud and emphatic thank you to the students who submitted to our book. When we put out the call for submissions, our inbox was flooded with amazing work, from alumni, transfers, current students, and everyone in between. The enthusiasm these writers and artists showed is what really bolstered this book into creation, and the journal we've ended up with is nothing short of beautiful. To all the writers and artists who submitted, thank you for sharing your work with us. And to all the other students and alumni who supported this book on its journey, thank you – without our community, this work couldn't exist. A special thank you goes out to Lexi Malone, for her help with graphic design and with our cover.

Lastly, we wanted to say thank you to the staff and faculty at SFUAD. Your support, guidance, insight, and enthusiasm was so valuable, and we couldn't have done this without you. We'd like to extend a special thank you to Julia Goldberg, for being our anchor as we figured all this complicated stuff out.

When SFUAD closed, a lot of students felt like they had lost their footing. The anger and frustration and abandonment we felt is all very real and alive in this edition of Glyph, but we hope that seeing all this artwork woven together can serve as a reminder that SFUAD is still here. The amount of gratitude and pride we feel with this book before us comes from the unforgettable group of students who lost their school but not their heart. Institutions may fail us, but a community can't die, and Glyph is here to symbolize that. The love between everyone at SFUAD is real, and we are here, and we wanted to give you one last reminder of that.

With love,

Brianna Neumann
Brandon Brown
Madeleine Sardina
Kylie Yockey

Don't Call the Bomb a Mother

MELINDA FREUDENBERGER

Looking into the morning-mirror, my face is smudged just outside the edges with sleep. I am slow to re-define: twist the mascara wand, push up and curl. The black is staining just above the lash. I look more like my mother than ever. She is the soot on my eyelid, she is the end of the world. Take her all off. Do it again.

I am on my knees in front of the moon. She is so big, yellowed and full of holes. She doesn't look at me because she doesn't have to. *Please tell me where my desire comes from.* I am begging, but she sucks the words right out of me. My high heat, my influenza, my fever. The hyper-need in my gut melts through my stomach and into the ground.

In the kitchen, I can't help but think of her: how did it feel—head buried in the oven's heat, the brain bursting back into space. A hand pushes through the daydream to touch my forehead, a soft *oh, you're burning up.* Close the oven door. Shut off the stove. Please walk away. My mother, the moon, pulling me back, telling me *not just yet*, telling me *go lie down.*

2

City History in August

MARISA DOHERTY

Once upon a hurricane eve, in a hole-in-the-wall Tex-Mex restaurant usually reserved for first dates and family parties of ten, I wrote snippets of my novel in a torn-up, eco-friendly notebook and avoided watching the news. My memories are so smeared with sweat and adrenaline that now I cannot untangle them any more than this, counting down to a blur of hot cars and hot houses and the audible train sound of tornados just outside. As an eve blossoms into hurricane landfall, I'm in my house, ticking toward midnight. This is my third hurricane, but this time I don't tell anyone I love them, not like last time, when I forwarded stupid chain messages to my entire class, including the boy who laughed and called me a lesbo at lunchtime, who thought he saw something in me I hadn't seen myself.

Get in the closet, the news anchor says. It's three a.m., and Channel 2 is on. Maybe I am drinking margaritas in the restaurant while the other patrons sink past tipsy and start singing. Or maybe I'm in bed, pressed shaking into the mattress while tornado warnings blow up my phone. *Why didn't you evacuate,* Facebook screams. The city is a memory of the last hurricane, of three million people spilling out onto highways in a mass exodus that claimed more lives than the storm itself, and after fourteen hours of sitting in a hot car in grid-locked traffic in hundred degree heat, there are no words, only numb horror for buses that explode and children run over and teenagers who have heart attacks in their cars. Collectively, we swore — *never again, we will never do this again, we will never leave again.* We kept our word through flood after flood, always thinking this is the end of it and now it has to stop because the odds are in our favor.

Welcome to another five-hundred-year storm.

These are the emergency numbers, the news anchor says just before there's a tiny explosion and the neighborhood electricity flickers out. I peek out the window at what was once a street and what is now a rushing river that looks so much like the river I floated in two weeks ago, proud, tan shoulders, strong swimmer, and the water is so close to the house now. Like captains in ships, we are drowning in beds and cars, and the water is ever-rising. I hide my face again. Alone in a bed in a hot dark house in a sodden city that prays for an end but cannot imagine what the end will look like when the flood recedes.

It is days, weeks, before it fully recedes, and the city is haunted by lakes and dams and rivers that were once streets. Drywall piles high on the corners, and two weeks later, we jog at the bayou and mark where the water rose forty feet over the embankment and spilled into the park. My house didn't even flood, so why does every morning bring another breathless moment, another fraction of a second before my mind catches up to the present, when I am still stuck in the moment before the hurricane and I'm filling bathtubs and stockpiling dollar water bottles and staring at empty grocery shelves and still so scared.

All the hashtags and slogans and donations cannot undo what has already happened, cannot fix the paralysis that strikes at a city whose people have waded out of their homes in chest-high water and whose people still wait on help that is slow to come and start to lose faith help will ever come at all. This wasn't the only hurricane to devastate this season, not by a long shot. I might be lighting matches on the name Harvey to burn it from my memory, but elsewhere, people are setting fire to Irma and Maria, to burn those away, too, and we are all failing.

There is a scream stuck in my throat because there are ghosts under every underpass, and only some of them are imaginary.

During Psychosis
SCHUYLER HALL GILMORE

They touch without fingers, their silent
seeking stares grazing along the curve of
my leg, up my thigh, these mist-like
apparitions that whisper
white-noised lullabies—

Fill me with fear. Fill me with
anger, with sadness, with anything
you'd like as long as it will be
enough to give me feeling,

because there's a void beneath my mask,
a hollow where it festers like disease—

carefully, they pull the threading until
every part of me is exposed,

that ugly, ugly girl, smiling back at me
from the mirror.

Church Grim
MADELEINE SARDINA

There was a funeral today. A burn victim from one of the wildfires that's had the town in a dusty haze for over a week. He didn't live here, but his mother did and he's buried next to her in one of the last available plots of carved-out earth. When the funeral-goers leave, marching out in their slow, slouched wave, I sit on the freshly filled grave and wait for the sun to set. Their grief makes them blind to me, or perhaps the translucence of my skin in the sunlight or the headstone with my name on it that marks an untouched plot at the entrance of the cemetery. Regardless, no one spares me a glance when I sit cross-legged on the turned soil and wait for sundown.

Tonight, hours after the moon has taken to the sky, what remains of the dead seeps out of the soil. It is soft, the soul, and too vulnerable for sunlight. I watch the first silver glint of it bubble up out of the dirt, a tiny spring of liquid mercury. I dip my hands beneath the soil, leaving it undisturbed in the wake of my nothingness, and when I lift my cupped palms again, all I bring with me is the pool of soul. I raise it up to eye level, feeling the life that was.

The first soul I tended to, centuries ago, was a man of fifty, a cobbler. I knew him. My mother and I shared a pew with him once, in Saint Mark's Church, the edifice that shades the cemetery. I stared down at his soul when it trickled up through the mound of dirt. I watched it shine for hours, still so unsure of my role in this dead world. When the sun stretched over the horizon, the soul began to bubble and steam and, in a panic, I stuffed my hands into the dirt and scooped out what I could. "Hello?" I asked the soul, my voice a tattered whisper. "Do you know where you're supposed to go?"

The soul grew warm, almost too hot, and melted between my fingers into nothing. There was a great gust of wind that nearly yanked the infant beech tree up by its roots, and then the air was still. The soul moved on. I felt the knowledge of it in my hands.

Those are the words I say to this younger soul, born nearly three hundred years after the first one. I whisper the words and the soul melts away to a place I have never been. This is my duty, has been since the consecration of the church and the cemetery. I am the first gatekeeper, a sign pointing, "That way." I sit alone on peaceful nights, waiting.

There is a girl propping her bicycle against the fence that wraps around the lopsided cemetery. It's midnight, or past it based on the low arching path of the gibbous moon, and the church has been silent for hours. She's dressed in dark colors, ripped denim, with a jagged slash of dark bangs that tumbles out of her ponytail. I know her. I've seen her after mass — she's the one who wears the same pale blue dress with the black canvas shoes every week. I've seen Father Leon scold her for her refusal to wear more appropriate shoes in the Lord's house, but each week she returns looking the same. Some days she wears a headband to pull back her unruly bangs, but she always takes it off by the time mass has ended. It leaves those bangs even worse for wear, fluffed up in the front and catching on her eyelashes. Yes, I've seen her before. But she, like anyone else, couldn't possibly see me.

"Hello," she whispers, pressing her stomach to the top bar of the old wooden fence and leaning over. "Can you speak?"

There's a tingling in my fingertips. There's a racing in my chest. I feel too corporeal, more than I have in centuries, and I'm not sure if I quite like the feeling. I don't have time to decide, however, because just then she hops the fence and creeps cautiously towards me. I see in one hand a notebook, in the other a flashlight, and a pencil tucked behind her ear. I stand from my position on the man's new grave and touch the headstone, grounding myself in the reality of cold granite and dirt. "My name is Joanna."

I feel my jaw work soundlessly for a second. How long has it been since I've spoken? "Margaret."

The sounds come out separate and hesitant. *Mar-ga-ret.* My voice is hoarse and crackling and sounds a bit like I spoke into the mouth of a cave, but she beams when I say my name and hurries forward a few more steps. I stumble back, putting the headstone between us. "I knew it," she says softly. "I knew you were — what are you? A ghost or someone's soul or something?"

I don't know how to answer her, so instead I ask, "How can you see me?"

She stops in her pursuit, toes inches from the foot of the grave. "Does no one else see you?"

I shake my head and am relieved when she also seems troubled by this. "Oh. I tried to ask my mom about you before, but she just ignored me. Or I *thought* she ignored me."

"You saw me before?" I ask.

"Sunday after mass. Actually, every Sunday for almost a month now. You're always under the beech tree."

She points to the tree in the center of the cemetery. I want to hide beneath its branches again. She wedges the flashlight under her armpit and plucks the pencil from behind her ear. "So your name is Margaret," she says, scrawling something in her notebook. "Are you buried here? Or, sorry — you are dead, yeah?"

She looks at me, waiting for an answer, and I contemplate becoming angry. I wonder what kind of fear I could strike into her. I've never tried to make anyone afraid of me. I've never had the chance.

"I'm dead," I answer, still too unaccustomed to the sound of my own voice to put any rage into it. "But I'm not buried in this cemetery."

"Oh?" She writes something else down. "Then why are you haunting it?"

I laugh — I didn't know my lungs could still push out a laugh — surprised at the idea of haunting anything. "I don't haunt," I tell her. "I'm a...guide of sorts."

"Oh."

This time the word is reverential and her eyes are wide and shiny in the moonlight. Something stirs in my stomach at the sight of such wonder, directed at me of all things. I step out from behind the headstone, hands clasped behind my back. "I'm not sure I should answer your questions," I tell her. "What will you use my answers for?"

"Research," she says quickly. "Just for my own knowledge, really. I'd be stupid not to ask the town ghost some questions."

The way she says *town ghost* makes me wonder, "Are there others who want to know about me?"

She hesitates, her eyes flickering to the headstone. "I don't know if they know about you," she says, "but there are plenty of old ghost stories around here, you know? People think the church is haunted. Sometimes there's weird noises in the chapel, like animals crying or something. A guy at my school says he saw a giant dog at the altar when he was in there alone."

There's a chill on the back of my neck. I take another step toward Joanna, toes turning the fresh earth of the grave. "Why are you here at night if this place is haunted?"

Joanna gestures at me, a smirk on her lips. "You just answered your own question." I stare a moment longer and her grin fades. "Everyone already thinks I'm strange. Letting them see me talk to myself in a graveyard wouldn't help that."

"Strange?"

"Yeah, you know. Just don't fit in."

I remember the way Father Leon scolds her about her Sunday clothing. "Because of what you wear."

Joanna laughs, her cheeks darkening with color. "No, but thanks. I'm just new in town. Mom and I moved here a couple months ago. We move a lot so I'm used to being sort of an outcast at school, but I'm not trying to make it worse."

There's an echo of something in my ear — an old fear, brought back by this girl's strangeness. "I see." I consider her again, flashlight still tucked beneath her arm and pencil poised, now a bit more shyly, over her notebook. "Well. Then I suppose I can answer your questions."

When I step closer to her, she doesn't back away. Her eyes rove over my bare feet, my nightgown, my thin, pale hair that was ghostly even before my death. I tuck a few strands behind my ear. "Sorry," Joanna says, meeting my eyes. "You're just… very young. How old are you exactly?"

It's been three hundred years since I died on the altar of Saint Mark's Church. Age is no longer a thing I know. "Come with me," I say.

The entrance of the cemetery is guarded by great iron gates that seem entirely unnecessary in the wake of the modest wooden fence that wraps around the rest of the land. The graves don't move chronologically or in any real order. There is a smattering of headstones dating back to the eighteenth century mixed among clusters of those from the twenty-first. But the first headstone, the one that christened the land, greets every visitor on the way in. "'Margaret McCloud,'" Joanna reads. "'Born May 5th, 1708. Died April 24th, 1724.' Jesus, you weren't even sixteen when you died."

She's looking at the headstone with strangely wounded eyes, like she's mourning her own death. I wonder how much older than sixteen she could possibly be.

"I thought you said you weren't buried here," she says after a moment, squatting in front of the headstone.

"I'm not. This marks an empty grave. My body is… elsewhere."

She looks at me then, and I see the conflict on her face as she decides to ask —

"Where is elsewhere?"

I trip my fingers over the top of the headstone, toying with the idea of telling her, and then I raise my hand, pointing at the church.

When I woke in the new cemetery, soil freshly baptized with innocent blood, I was beneath the spindly branches of the young beech tree. It was night still, or maybe night again, and I had a new ache above my heart. I rubbed my sternum to push the feeling away and stood, walking on unsteady legs back to the church where the lamplights still flickered.

I peered in through the window to the sanctuary. The stained glass clouded my vision, but I saw robed men — deacons and Father Alistair. Cold panic clawed up my veins, vague memories of prayers and blood. They bundled something dark and dripping in white cloth and shoved it into a gaping hole in the floor of the sanctuary. "Board it up," Father Alistair said. "No one can know where she rests."

When the deacons moved to fetch the boards, I saw my own face, bloodless and vacant, staring back at me from beneath the altar.

Joanna leaves, sickly pale and trembling. I watch her go, knowing she'll be back — hoping she'll be back. I spend the following day wondering if I should have lied and told Joanna I was just another lost soul buried peacefully. Perhaps that would have drawn her back.

But she returns anyway.

"We should take things slow with the questions," she says, sitting down with me beneath the beech tree. "Last night was…intense."

So she asks me about my life rather than my death. She wants to know what it was like being a young woman in the eighteenth century, what it was like to be a settler in a new town, who my family was. I told her about my mother. "She was a widow," I say, sitting cross-legged and facing Joanna like a mirror. "We came to this town when I was very young, too young to remember. She wanted us to start a new life without the memories of my father following us, and a new town felt like the best place to do that. But since no one here knew her, there were nasty rumors about the nature of my conception and whether or not she had actually ever been married. She had many men proposition her, telling her they could make all the rumors go away. But she told me she had already tied herself to a man and had no intention of doing so again, so she never remarried."

"My mom's a single mom too," Joanna says. "Divorced, though, not widowed. She doesn't like to talk about it because everyone at church gives her dirty looks for it."

I hear that echo again — my mother's voice, my name. *Not her, not my Margaret! Please, take me instead!*

"That's wise of her," I tell Joanna.

She comes back every night after that. She asks a question each time — bland inquiries about my life, about my existence as a guide for souls. Never about my death. Her eyes reveal how much she wants to know, and how afraid she is of the answer. I'm not sure I could tell her even if she asked.

"Am I the first to ever see you?" she asks on the fifth night. "Am I special? Or does this happen, like, every hundred years or something?"

"This has never happened before," I tell her honestly. "I haven't spoken to anyone since I died."

"So why me?" Joanna asks. She's laying down, belly on the cool earth beneath the tree, head resting on her arms.

I hesitate, looking at Joanna's hands. Her fingernails are painted a shiny red. I reach out to touch the glossy surface, wondering if I would wear such a color had I been born in a different time. When my fingertip grazes hers, there is a spark and we both recoil. She looks at me, cradling her hand to her chest now. "I think," I tell her, "we are very similar."

I sit beneath the beech tree three days later, watching the congregation arrive for Sunday mass. Joanna is with her mother, wearing the same pale blue dress and black canvas shoes. As they walk along the fence line, she looks over at me. I feel more spectral than usual when she sees me, and I raise a hand for a half wave in an attempt to appear more human. She doesn't wave back, of course, but she smiles and then looks back to her mother. I try a smile on my own face. It feels new.

Father Leon remains outside the church watching the last of the congregation trickle out. He bears a passing resemblance to Father Alistair and I wonder, not for the first time, if some distant relative of my old priest lives in this man. Something in the eyes says so.

An older woman, veiled in black, rises from her seat on one of the benches outside and approaches him. He holds one hand out, nearly as wrinkled as hers, and she clasps it tight, trembling visibly even from where I stand. She says something to him, and I realize that she's crying, grieving, and the smell of the wildfires in the air thickens for a moment. Father Leon nods and I hear what he says as if he whispered the words directly into my ear: "We'll consecrate the new cemetery for him, sister."

※

I sit in front of my headstone, staring at the words that mark nothing. The tips of my fingers and toes tingle, yearning for a warmth they'll never feel again. Joanna will come tonight. She must.

"Margaret!"

The name falls on my skin like a blanket, Joanna's young voice as soft as the soil underneath me. Her quiet footfalls stop. "Margaret," she says again, quieter now.

"Not her, not my Margaret! Please, take me instead!"

The memory presses against my sternum, filling the space where my heart once pulsed. I am here and there, between my headstone and this girl, between the two men dragging me from my home. Their hands are tight on my arm, bruising and uncaring. I know them. I saw them beside Father Alistair performing mass, consecrating the new land for the church and the neighboring cemetery. The hem of my nightgown catches around my ankles, tangling me in the soft cotton. "What do you want?" My voice is choked, pleading, but they don't listen.

"I want to know how you died," Joanna tells me now. "I'm ready."

I can see them hunting through her house. I can see them rip back her sheets, plunder her closet and under her bed. I can see them realize she is not home and then I feel them return.

They hold my limbs to the four points of the altar, wrapping coarse rope around my wrists and ankles. Father Alistair paces the stone block, watching me struggle in vain, and then he places his palm on my forehead. "Merciful God," he says, "you sent your son to save us, to take our sins and lead us to life everlasting."

"Margaret?" Joanna says my name again, this time reaching out. When her fingertips graze my arm, a flurry of goosebumps rises to my elbow. Another spark, more powerful than the first time we touched, winds its way up her arm. She jumps back, startled and hurt.

I can't tell if the tingling in my fingertips is from her touch or Father Alistair's words. When he pulls out a large knife from his robes, my vision narrows to his hand clenched at the hilt. He presses the point to my chest where my heart pounds, betraying its own position. "Please accept this sacrifice that we may find our own way to you."

"Do you know where you're supposed to go?" I ask her, my voice nearly drowned in the invocation of my memory.

"What?"

Behind her, the shrouded men approach. Father Leon stands in the doorway of the church. My body rots beneath the altar. I cup my hands and reach into her chest.

There was a funeral today. A young girl, not yet sixteen, was found collapsed in the cemetery two nights ago, dead of a heart attack. There is no room in the cemetery of Saint Mark's Church, so they take her to Saint Joseph's a few towns over. The procession is small — only a hearse and a lonesome car with one weeping woman. Father Leon stands on the church steps and watches them go. Tonight is peaceful. I sit beneath the beech tree and wait.

The Ocean Doesn't Love Me Back
JUDITH RIPLEY

with water filled lungs
and a jellyfish stung tongue
i continue to drown

Control
KYLIE YOCKEY

Do you think you could handle the way
I manhandle your
heart hips hands around
my waist in my arms—
I've taken bites out of thighs
with thicker skin than you;
and are you under the impression
that getting under me
would take you to the top
of my priorities?
Let me relieve you of your
misunderstanding:
I understand nothing
of loving
tenderly.
I only know how to skin you down,
release after sweet release,
until you're relieved
when I release you.

And Soften the Limbs They Touch
ANDREW KOSS

It is midnight at The Fountain Club. A swelling tide of revelers rise and fall along the apron of the stage, but Marley sits alone. His high school Letterman jacket is a reassuring hand to his back. Two men take the seats beside him and pull each other close. Marley forces himself down in his seat. A loosely gripped bottle of golden apple cider drips beads of sweat in his palm.

Sizzling cymbals jostle his senses. On stage, a smooth leg, milky and waxen, kicks out from the wings. Gold cords form a lattice along a lean calf, terminating in a tan leather sandal on the sole of the foot. It steps softly onto the stage, accompanied by spritely Mellotron runs. At the apex of an organ crescendo, Nerissa leaps onto the runway. She is lithe beneath her white linen chiton. Marley's eyes flutter, following the floating hem of the dancer's garment. It ends mid-thigh, a dizzying display that taunts him.

Nerissa is Sal Wasserman's stage name. He was a year behind Marley at James Buchanan High. But with a coat of midnight blue splashing her lips, they are strangers on the shore. She pirouettes and springs across the stage. A wreath of blonde plaits bounces against her bare shoulders. Her arms slink over her hips, coming to rest beneath a modest foam bust that fills out the folds of her tunic. She embraces herself as Peter Gabriel's vocals saturate Marley's eardrums.

She slips to her knees and rolls her abs with the unrelenting eddies of Phil Collins' drum fills. Then she presses her palms against the runway's plywood panels and raises her hips. Marley shifts his seat closer to the stage. As the music accelerates, Nerissa rises to her feet and spins. The gold rope tied round her waist whizzes above Marley's head.

Nerissa's cheeks sparkle as the stage lights catch the beveled edges of sequins adhered to her skin. She keeps her eyes closed, expertly executing steps from memory, the dimensions of the runway mapped in her mind. In her high school bedroom, Sal recreated each inch of The Fountain stage. She can practically feel the shag carpet wisp between her toes. There, Sal exorcised his daily demons, stepping into a ring to perform a fighter's regimen. His feet struck the floor, preparing for the day when the sway of his hips would invite applause instead of bruises.

It was Marley, one afternoon, who caught Sal in the halls of Buchanan High. "Why you walk like a bitch?" he yelled, grabbing Sal at the waist and pulling him into the men's room. He hoisted Sal by the collar and threw him into a bathroom stall, where he smashed his mouth against a toilet's porcelain rim. The janitor spent an hour cleaning blood off the tiles. Two visits to the dentist and seventeen hundred dollars later, Sal finally felt comfortable opening his mouth to smile again.

It is a washed out memory in Marley's mind, forgotten amidst many other similar encounters. The swirling vortex of Nerissa's hips, once the target of so much rage, now hold Marley hypnotized. The swing of her ilia opposes his denial. In the ascending heights of a guitar solo, she rakes her nails across her chest. She opens her eyes a fraction of an inch and squints to peer through a pool of light. In this moment, Marley is sure he has been seen.

She lies on the runway for the song's finale. Moonbeams shower through the skylight, luminescing her pallid skin. With one knee raised, she exposes her thigh in Marley's direct line of sight. A signal, he thinks. The song's final chord erupts, and Nerissa rises to her feet. She curtsies and blows a kiss to the audience.

Marley has no gesture to offer in return, so he wades through the crowd of clamoring men to claim a spot at the bar. He rests his butt halfway on a stool, and turns to Jadon, the bartender. "Does Nerissa usually come out after the show?" Marley asks, eying the stage.

"Sometimes," Jadon says, filling a glass with laurel green liquid. "Why? You her boyfriend?"

"What does she like to drink?"

"Amaretto. On the rocks."

"Get me one of those," Marley says, placing a twenty on the counter. "And another cider." His gaze still trained on the crowd, he seeks out strings of gold, or pale cheeks, or loose garments that promise to share a secret.

Nerissa enters from a side door behind the bar, still in costume but for her black leggings and a light jacket draped over her shoulders. She lights a cigarette. Jadon beckons her with a curling finger. "Chaser," he whispers, then perches himself on the back counter. He pulls out a towel and wipes the inside of an already dry mug.

Nerissa adjusts her wig and takes a drag of her cigarette. She's off the clock. She could leave. She could just go home and read. A straight man's devotion expires faster than a mayfly. Nevertheless, she circles around the bar, then stops suddenly. The prominent penciled crescents of her eyebrows arch higher. There is Marley Blair, unkempt sideburns trailing from his temples like rope. She struggles not to drown in a whirlpool of the past. Here he is, at The Fountain Club, where she'd never before had reason to look over her shoulder. But even here, the word "safety" is just a placebo. The Fountain has no more mystical capacity to conceal her than the slatted refuge behind the bleachers at Buchanan High. For a moment, she considers slipping behind an artificial tree at the corner of the bar, but it is too late. She has been seen.

"You wanted me?" she asks.

Marley's smile is an aura, a stone thrown, ringing ripples in Nerissa's mind: when a chorus gave Sal's desires a name, a projectile that hit him in the gut before he could ascertain its weight, its shape; when lingering on the banks of convention drew the piercing arrows of the pure; when the painted face he admired in the mirror or the affirming drape of a homemade skirt was deemed permission to trespass, to lay bare, to take his measure and answer the question of what he "really had down there."

"You look smaller," Marley says.

Nerissa's lacquered lips form a crest in her dimpled cheek. Back to punish me some more, she thinks. He still wears the same oversized jacket, with their high school's crest, that he should have gotten rid of two years ago. He still has the hole beneath his mouth where a lip ring used to be, like someone hooked him and threw him back.

"I mean, smaller than you did on stage," Marley says. "Here, I got you a drink."

He nudges the glass toward Nerissa, who confirms that Jadon is still close at hand before taking a seat. Marley rests his hand on her knee, a light caress on polyester-lycra. She expects a crushing fist, a bone-clenching grip, but his fingers gently brush her thigh with a repetition that irritates her skin.

"You were mesmerizing," he says, gazing at her over the lip of a bottle. She is the spirit to whom he will sacrifice his skin. "Can I take you somewhere?" he asks.

Where, like a bathroom stall or something?

"Where would you like to go?"

The twisted tubes of a neon sign diffuse the angles of Marley's cheeks. His arms are hairless, she observes, not the wiry nest of fur she remembers. And there's a fresh, olive scent about him instead of the vinegar stench of locker room sweat. He steps off of the stool, treading closer, and squeezes her thigh. He slips his fingers beneath her skirt. "I never thought I could catch you," he whispers.

"How long have you been thinking about this?" she asks, swirling the amber liquid in her glass. Did he know he would find her here? Perhaps, some years ago, Marley came upon him in the frigid stalls of the gym class showers. Perhaps a passive wish awoke then that he couldn't put to sleep. Sal always hurried to be the first one into the showers and the first one out. But there was a time, prior to their bathroom rendezvous, when he would linger, hoping that Marley might enter before he could finish. Perhaps he needed curtains to frame these cheeks, Nerissa thinks, as she twirls the ends of her nylon hair.

But Marley sees nothing familiar in her eyes. He never dove so deep inside them before tonight. The fluorescent sign buzzes above them. Nerissa thinks of winged insects, induced to comply with their own destruction. She crushes the butt of her cigarette in an ashtray and sets her glass back on the counter. As the club lights dim, strobes and lasers power up and rain vibrant patterns across Marley's face. A beautiful glow, she thinks.

Then Marley strikes, flicking his tongue past her lips before she can recoil. He wraps his arm around her neck and slides his hand beneath the collar of her jacket. He's already decided he can have me, she thinks, as Marley's feelers clutch her shoulder. She struggles to free herself from his embrace.

"It's alright," he says, and leads her to the dance floor. He grabs her by the waist and shoves his hips against her. They are pressed so close, it's like Marley is trying her on. Waves of bass crash around them as Marley's hand comes to rest at the small of her back. Go with it, she thinks. Let him think he's won. She channels the charms of her on-stage persona, merging with Marley and swaying in sync.

What happens when he unwraps me? she thinks. Which parts should I conceal? How long can I keep my forms on? It will be over before it's begun. But Marley hasn't planned that far ahead. His thoughts are absorbed with her. He presses his forehead against her lips and says, "You feel so real."

Jadon clears his throat, still watching from the bar, but Nerissa waves him away. She grabs Marley's sandpaper jaw. "You want to see something?" she asks.

Marley grins.

She tongues the sores that grow worse every time she eats. She opens her mouth and undoes the plastic clasps hugging the edge of her gums. Then she pulls out her partial dental bridge, leaving behind an amorphous cavern of tender, soft tissue. A string of saliva falls from her lip.

"This is real," she says.

For the Trees, Before They Chopped Me Down
BRIANNA NEUMANN

My chest-cage softened itself
as you spread on your broad bark-curved back.
I never imagined your sweet-leaf breath
so clustered close to me,
a closeness I could want, and
I never dreamt I could believe
wicker eyes and wander smile,
goldness, goodness, newness;
a boy, or man, with simple body, strange
lack of strangeness, and the easy whisper
of myself against summer hands, so much larger
than my own. My lungs
were paper parchment and I curled
my toes so near I sensed your innocence,
the billow significance and flicker forgotten
of your heart's meatiness —
you wanted the flame of me against your paleness,
an aspen boy with sides disassembled,

stories and cigarettes huddled,
the beer-drunk of my wobble and clutter.
I always thought I had a penchant for waifs
but you are a wafer, straight, unnibbled,
a gentle
       lovely
            unmarked
                      quiet space.

Almost Ready
KYLIE YOCKEY

So maybe I still want to kiss you?
Maybe I miss your every touch?
Maybe my teeth beg to sink maybe my bed cuddles cold—
but I believe in mind over body
and my brain is just waiting for my muscles
to lose their memory.

A Letter to Spalding Gray
BONNIE BEE

Spalding,

I wonder: Are you my father? Nothing as commonplace as genes or blood relations, but the kind of father who you meet in the fabric of the universe.

Or are you my lover? Because that's the next logical leap, of course, my father always wanted me to be with a man like him and (unfortunately) that has rubbed right off onto my subconscious, so I'm wondering as I'm watching your face, could you be my lover, had we been spurted into this world around the same time—and I love to be wanted.

I loved you from the moment I first heard you speak. So many parts of me for so long were like that multivitamin you have to take every morning—it's something that keeps happening, and you have to do it, but god, the smell, the taste, the way it sticks to your throat going down.

Was it only me who experienced those things, or was it me and other people as a whole, or was it me and a smaller selection of people, and did it matter at all?

But you taught me that the tangled and rotting roots of my family tree, the polluted fruit and gnarled branches could actually be very good writing material. And my dark thoughts, my mental illness could incite not only empathy, but laughter of relating—which means I'm not alone, and that's kind of important to me. I'm not sure why. I like spending time alone.

After hearing my first Spalding monologue, I became obsessed with your whole body of work. I decided in the American Go-For-It Spirit I would travel to any corner of the country to attend one of your shows to experience the crackle of energy at full volume that I could only get a sense of when watching you on television.

I was checking for your next speaking engagement, looking for a website where I could find your next great work—but what caught my eye was an article from the Times: *Body of Spalding Gray Found; Monologist and Actor Was 62*.

No.

In several hours, I read through the last three years of your life until my brain felt too big for my head. These detached reports of your disappearance carelessly broke my heart, the soft snap and crumble of chalk underfoot, and I wept.

And I'm with you in North Haven, where the dog is already howling for the late Spalding Gray, a Chekhovian lamentation, and every day your thoughts of suicide rise like a black sun in your sky.

I'm with you in Soho, where you leave your wallet on a kitchen countertop in your loft, a tome of official earthly documents that you won't need where you're going. God has your rap sheet.

I'm with you on the East River, where you split the heavens above the Staten Island Ferry, and in my dreams you walk from the Greenpoint shore where you washed up, dripping from a sea-journey back to your mother.

I hope you wore a coat that night.

May I call you Spald? I always liked the name; it suited you much more than Spalding, but that's what everyone always announced you as, and I'm a little bit preoccupied with formality.

Yours,

BB

Sea Maiden

KELSEY MARIE MOGHADASPOUR

My name means Dweller at a Ship Island. I am the ship island, luring boats closer and closer until I drown them in my waters. Dark, cold, relentless; I am the storm that pushes you to me for shelter. Both the safety you feel, and the nightmare that paralyzes you, I am the enigma that may never be solved. Larger than life, but made smaller by those who disparage me. I am the waves, full of power and crashing down onto my shores where I collect things from the oceans surrounding me. Humans throw their sorrows into the sea: broken engagements, heartbreak, the death of a loved one, the dreams they once had that crashed down around them. And they float, all alone, in the water for me to find. Small treasures, they are. My only taste of the human lives that are just past my shores. For I have exposed all that I am worth with nothing to show. I have broken my back time and time again to collect these small human treasures. So be wary. Get caught in my currents, try to take my gems from me, and I will show no mercy.

Nicked
KYLIE AYN YOCKEY

My nectar blooms in dewy petals
from my flower mound
and streaks red down my stems

In the Days After the Storm has Passed
LINDSEY TOWNSEND

1.

I cried today,
over you,
for the first time in a month.
Contemplated texting you
for the fifth time today,
the tenth time this week, but I
stop myself.
Tell myself *I'm over this*, when the sun
is shining, but once it sets
and the cold dark
creeps in, and I look
at the pictures
I have still not deleted
from my phone, and
I remember the deep ache
I felt the morning you left,

the morning you sent that
text: "I'm a better person
for having met you…"
you said. That day
my heart turned into an angry
red bird that begged to fly
out of my chest, frantically
trying to escape, it rattled
my ribcage and left me gasping.

I tell myself, I'm over this.
But I compose
a message. Leave it
in drafts. I lay there
and look at the inky darkness
that spreads itself like a stain
across my bedroom ceiling.
I try to stop imagining
your face.

2.

I cried over you, today, for the first time in two months.
The hot water of my shower pounding at my shoulders,
as hotter tears slide down my cheeks. Last night, I dreamt that you
weren't okay. Dreamt you'd let yourself go. Saw you bloated
and aching; saw you in tears on your bathroom floor. I woke up
with a desperate panic in my chest and felt sure
you must be struggling. I woke up scared for you. You,
the quiet boy that is no longer in my life. So I sat in the shower.
I let the tears come. I let the water turn cold.

3.

Today I cried gentle tears over you,
as I sat in the nest of pillows and blue blankets that is my bed.
Because finally, after months, after everything—after dreams,
and nightmares, after aching and hoping and hurting.
I think of you,
and feel nothing.

Honey
CHANTELLE MITCHELL

He stands in front of me, half-naked. Hips with honeyed skin. Watches me as I watch him. There are plenty of other things I'd rather eat, and he knows this. Though the small patch of stretch marks on his inner thigh makes my tongue clench, a trail of thick hair leads to his pinkish half-hard on, which isn't there for me, and makes me spit up the saliva pooling in my mouth; it lands in his navel. I look down where the thick sugar is running onto his knees, and see his skin is lost under zigzags of knotted leg hair and maybe lint. I had thought, from the way his stomach always stretched his shirts out, that he'd be bigger, but it turns out he actually just wears clothes that are two sizes too small and I'm disappointed because there's less of him to hold onto than I anticipated. Naked, he looks saggy, which might be why he drenches himself in my favorite honey—the one I use on my pancakes. I want to tell him that it won't tighten his pendulous skin. But his ears, fat and blushing, can't hear me.

A fly buzzes by and gets stuck in the wet dimples of his thigh but he still licks his lips. He looks at me expectantly, as if he thinks I'll do the same. Neither the fly nor I are as in love with him as he is, though. He picks up the creature by its twitching wings and strings of sweet gold stretch tight and twinkle in the morning sunlight. Outside, the neighborhood is quiet, each house dealing with its own sticky, furry, self-obsessed man in its own way. The sun is rising loudly this morning, a sizzling from the sky as the leaves crinkle dry and fall. All the moisture this town can afford is in this room with me as I screw up my face and he studies the fly for moments before crushing it between his fingers.

Without cleaning off the guts, he goes back to exploring his own hips and sighing contently. I leave to get something that'll help me prepare for what's coming, that'll help me wash it down. Milk or maybe mint tea. I spend as much time as I can out of his vicinity before he's searching for me and suctioning sticky footprints onto the hardwood. "Come on dear," he says in a gurgly voice, too lost in his own lust. "We are waiting." I gulp, knowing that I'm in trouble when he refers to himself as "we," since that means he'll be especially unbearable. I return to his room and take off my shirt, put on my gardening gloves.

He puts the standing mirror next to the bed so he can watch himself with sparkling eyes. I keep mine focused on the ceiling and kneel behind him as he gets on all fours. I move past his clenched ass cheeks and feel for his tender, honey-soaked balls, slowly peeling them apart and off his body. He moans his own name and a cluster of birds outside scatter and break off the chalky bits of roof from my little home. "I want to see them, let me see how gorgeous they are." He's groaning into the sheets and I lift them so he can see them in the mirror. Their wet noises are muted as I roll them around in my gloved hands. His body under me melts and melts until there's just a puddle of tacky liquid clinging to my floral sheets, like some goddess pissed the bed. The sun sets and I keep them in my tea cup.

Natural Predator
KYLIE AYN YOCKEY

'I will eat you'
said the mayfly to the frog
'I will devour your skin
And lay eggs in your lungs'

'I will redesign you'
it prodded again
'Your rapid tongue will not
Lash and your knees will live backwards'

the frog remains and the mayfly
crawls onto its juicy amber eye
'I will shrink you
And you will never meet the sun

And you will never bathe in mud
You will never bathe again'
it jams its own Argus eye into the mouth of the frog
glaring at the stomach contents inside

the frog opens wide

Pilgrimage
JACEY ELLIS

The field is a void. A skin stripping wind blows through the valley. The moaning air whips against the back of several fish-belly-white and hairless legs. There are people facing the middle of this space, waiting.

The Crone paces between the rows of people waiting in the chilling air, waving herb and smoke into the sky. The point of her black hood is snuffing out the stars. Her bones creak as though they are branches shaking against a certain wind.

Close to the center is a lake. It is a black mirror against the moon, reflecting the emptiness back into the sky. The moon is lonely here.

The congregation (they call themselves) divide into rows under the moonlight. The smallest bodies, the ones not chosen for ceremony, are in the front. A chubby boy with rotting fingernails jabs the baby girl in his mother's arms. The baby begins to wail as a breeze wrings the lake nearly dry, flicking water across the land and into the faces of the crowd. The mother hushes the baby's screams with a few pinches and jabs of her own. Her teeth are rotting. Her breath smells of dead crow left in the lake marsh.

The baby is forgotten against the growing glow of porcelain bodies in the night. Standing next to one another in a perfect line, twelve small female faces glitter against the solitary, unblinking star of the moon. The Crone removes a satchel from her waist, removes some of its contents, and blows dust onto each prepubescent chest.

Tears squeeze out of a terrified and shaking blue eye. Her nude, anchovy body sparkles with the bodies next to hers. They are similar and unmarked. One girl knocks her knee into the other and it echoes through the grass. One chest is peaked so hard against the cold rushing air and her hair is matted. Two others cough.

A father eyes his daughter's body and wonders if his upbringing was enough, wonders if he did good work in preparing her. His daughter's eyes do not find his as he carefully gazes upon her; she looks toward him only after he has turned to criticize the next girl in line. He gives them each the same consideration, as if they were all the same to him, as if he could not tell her from the other shaking silhouettes.

The pulsing darkness dampens its already heavy grip on the field and plunges it deeper into darkness. The dark is safe for the congregation. In the dark, everyone is the same.

From somewhere over the hills to the West, a drumming erupts out of the hum and glow of terror. Another small child moves to wipe a yellow and running nose with his tattered sleeve. He coughs phlegm into the crook of his arm. A solitary horned bull screams from a distant farm. The drumming grows louder, more frantic.

The bull wails. The congregation wails. The drumming hands wail.

Pushing against one another in anxious and building haste, the crowd begins to break their tight formations. Who will get to see first? Who will get to see best?

"Brothers and sisters," croaks the Crone, lost in the crowd. She pushes the hood from her face down against her cold, angled shoulders. Her face is that of a gargoyle; death, mangled with flesh and blood.

"The world," she says, "is hungry."

She licks her cracked lips. From them she tastes fear. A clawed, boney, and shaking hand extends toward the blackening sky. She bids it grow even blacker still. Her head tilts to meet the moon and a dry laugh becomes her throat. Her larynx will set the field ablaze.

She is conjuring flame and chaos.

Another drum joins the first and the field is suddenly vibrating.

Another man in the crowd removes his dirtied black hat by its torn brim. He smiles. His mouth is an abyss of broken teeth and a swollen, purpled tongue but he is a proud father to his family. His wife, smelling of pig rot, adjusts her lopsided and lump-filled breast. Their son wraps his mother's moth-eaten stole around his nearly-missing left ear.

In a moment of desperation, a girl amongst the twelve throws herself into the crowd. She is pushed back into place without a word by a boy her same age.

A woman without children or husband jeers and throws a handful of dry grass into the face of the smallest girl. The girl spits some blood into the dirt and licks the earth and salt from her tiny pink mouth.

The drumming is deafening. An eardrum bursts.

Something of a different earth, or perhaps a different time, lets a guttural moan roll through the valley. It rears beneath the congregation's feet and claws against deep earth to drink from the starless sky.

"My friends," screeches the Crone against the wind and tears and the wailing and the water and the bull and the sky, "for we know what we must sacrifice to the world when we are brought into it. And so, too, this must go." She reaches into the blackness and pulls a handful back down with her.

The drumming grows even louder as the earth begins to crack and boil.

The girls, twelve in strength and folly, kneel for their medicine.

Limbic Malfunction, Part Three

SCHUYLER HALL GILMORE

Yet—

Perhaps the demon never leaves you,
cannot be exorcised by sheer will alone—

and lingers in the mind, suckling like a child,
taunting you with its thirst, baiting you with its

memory. Like me, father, you wonder how to gratify the
growing hunger, how to douse its flame long enough

to live—

but the demon never sleeps, is never satisfied, and lurches—

we are possessed for life,

your red-rimmed eyes tell me: it is so.

To the Coyotes Outside the Bedroom Window of My Childhood Home
LINDSEY TOWNSEND

I listen as you cackle, coyote
cry, and I wonder if you
have any idea the way your conversations
contribute to the catastrophes that are
my dreams—the way they are capacious, feel like spiral, crash,
shake, stop. I hear you, as I close my eyes, concocting sleep, and then
I am running—running from your laughter, your snarled
face, white teeth, silent steps, tan hide—I try to run and hide—and I wonder
of your intentions. I wonder
if maybe your cries are, in some strange hidden way, protecting me
from something even bigger. Something deep within my dreams.
I wonder if this is you keeping my head above water.

Easily Digestible
CHELSEA NAPPER

The roiling of the boat from side to side feels endless, impotent, to these people who have huddled down into themselves. Waves pass beneath the faded wooden hull, slippery, almost refusing to support its weight.

To even so much as touch it.

In the vast nothingness in which they bob, these people have learned silence. The seconds all around them don't touch them, jostle them.

The seconds don't show their faces.

They pile up, separated and out of order, suspended about the boat as a mist. Disjointed time takes the place of air in lungs beset by water.

It chokes, blots out vision.

Separating the sightless passengers from the damp hastiness below, the ashen grey planks gradually disintegrate, soggy flakes carried away by the indifferent current.

There had once been a destination, a commonwealth hope for the vision of a bloodless tomorrow.

They fled foreign bullets found in their native beds.

Yet, the foreign shores at which these people aimed still cling, patriotically, to the rule fate. The drifters jilted their predisposition. They set sail for a place shrouded in the hazy, teal guise of freedom.

Erect in copper fist, beckoning torch never set ablaze.

Thusly, these huddled masses in their pulpy planks have been set adrift to roam, aid-less, in the mists of the foreign. They rot, barely above the surface. Their souls denied observance, until their faceless lights peep out from the sodden chunks of their vessels.

Iridescent, those lights draw attention.

They wash ashore to glitter blindly up into the faces of vacationing children, and muse-less portrait artists. Only then do those unseen of the refugee hoards earn their place in the land of the free. Only once their souls have become tragic enough to be commodified into art.

Made easily digestible.

Youth Retreat

JOSE ARAGUZ

On the second day, the counselor had the children write down any and all sins they carried with them in their thoughts, anything they had done or considered doing, then passed around a coffin made from a wastebasket. *Throw in your sins,* they were told, *so that your sinful selves can die.* Each child watched their hands join the other hands in writing, folding, crumpling. After the dying, each hand came back empty, but the words written and tossed remained fresh inside them still.

Pale Pink
KYLIE AYN YOCKEY

Egg shell rot
pours down my fore-
head under
a wreath of thorns
and bubblegum…
"Whore of Bethlehem"
whips and splashes,
passes,
through my ears and
eyes as I gaze paralyzed
out at the crowd.
I am Queen Carrie;
I'm slipping off the cross—

Infinity on High
(Fall Out Boy, 2007)
MARINA WOOLVEN

1.   Thriller

How easy it is to imagine the squealing of the car, desperate, against the scorch
of the street, the spin of the wheel like the whiplash of orbit—

and the passenger seat is empty but I pretend you're in it. I think of a voice beside
my own, that I am not alone, and I think of you slamming your head into the dash
again and again. I imagine when I hurl into the oncoming traffic and my skull cracks
in half, you meet the fractures one for one. I think of smoke and ash and the pulse
of your flinch, that

flicker

2.   The Take Over, the Breaks Over

This isn't fair, is what you say. I am still thinking of bodies on the side of the
road and the way the scent of smoke will linger and trace on for days, drags itself
after you. I'm wondering the best way to mourn. Nothing was ever fair. Do you
remember when we were in highschool, how the threat of school shootings were so

often that if we skipped each time there was one, we'd just never go to school and what life is that? What is it?

You went to school and did your work while flinching, learning to not blink. You always thought you'd be the first to go because you've always been so self centered, so much like the sun. It's all my fault. I've rotated around you for too long.

I went to school and lit fires in the bathroom because I could. I pressed saftey pins into the soft ears of my friends because I could. I never did think much about gunmen.

3.   This Ain't a Scene, It's an Arms Race

No one ever did come in shooting. The thing about a gunman is first come the arms dealer, then comes baby in the body bag.

You are too stupid to be afraid when you come home. When you cry I want to ask if you are giving up, except I don't really care whose side wins. I don't see sides. There are no sides. There is only you, still flinching into me, imploding like swell of the sky when the sun forgets how to rise and falls back down–

At midnight the trashcan glitters. The birds sing at the wrong time. These beautiful things I will not wake you for.

4.   I'm Like a Lawyer with the Way I'm Always Trying to Get You Off (Me & You)

The first time I woke up next to you, I didn't know what to think. The ceiling was dripping in stars and plastic and blue, tangled in your hair and it was night, and you were undoubtedly beautiful, cosmo-light face. In the day I was happy to learn how to get you off like it was our honeymoon. It wasn't our honeymoon. You were still sleeping, and I ached for water but you were on my legs pinning me down, did not let me up to get water and there for the first time, in that moment, hate–

5.   Hum Hallelujah

I wait in the car at the gas station while you go inside and put money on the pump, pick up your pack of cigarettes, your cheap candy that makes my teeth ache, make me want to reach in and rip them out. At the pump I see a man, at another pump, and from the glass of the store I see you looking back, and I'm looking back, and he's filling up his car. I think of running out and throwing my arms around him, promising him everything he ever wanted, promise to love him like no one else. I imagine being tucked away in the back seat, folded up, and never seeing you again as he drives me off. Better, I want to drag him by his coat onto the hood of our car and fuck him on top, you still watching from the other side of the glass, the streetlights in the night glaring down.

or   I consider walking out of our car, to him, cutting off his head and then walking into the store and slamming it onto the counter just to see what you'll do.

or   I consider cutting off his head, walking in, letting you stare long enough until you understand, you wouldn't even scream, and then cutting off yours.

or   I consider cutting off his head, walking in, presenting it to you, and then us kissing, us fucking, in love again, the head left on the counter watching.

But he is driving off. You are checking out.

I am so bad at these things.

6.   Golden

The mirror is melting, or you broke it. My feet are burning, or they are cut, and bleeding. I don't have a mirror anymore. You go outside and the sun is out. The atmosphere is thinner above your head, you think, skin burning. It follows you as you walk the neighborhood and you wonder if you only reached up, pressed into the blue, would that thin layer could crack beneath your palm like brittle ice; which way would you plunge?

You think *I wish I could hurl the world into the sun.*

7.   Thnks fr th Mmrs

I never believed in fortune tellers but when the crystal ball dropped and cracked I picked it up screaming, "Who? Who?"

That bitch didn't give me my money back. I went home to divine in your eye but I turned you cataract instead and we spent the rest of the night watching movies, or at least, I watched them and held you down with me. When we sleep our bed heaves in heavy breaths. Is this fate or habit? Is this the best you could do?

There are no sides, I've taught you. There is only the other. Look into me— I have your own face.

8.   Don't You Know Who I Think I Am?

You think the neighbors are noticing you. Your walks are getting longer on that smear of a street, the kind you could drown in. It's your favorite hobby, feeling sorry for yourself. Often I'm inside not cleaning but staring under the sink, the soap, the bleach, the ammonia, like dreams. I think a lot of killing you and then myself. I think of sheep, dancing.

9.   The (After) Life of the Party

We met when I was innocently trying to commit suicide. How many times did you imagine I was the one shot? Did you like the idea of dating the dead girl? I liked the idea of being one. But we were at the house of a friend during a party and it was inappropriate timing. You stopped me and then you gave me blunts, we smoked in the bathroom curled up in the tub. We got too high and I could see your blood cells swelling, bubbled fat under your skin. They pushed past your pores and floated up like red balloons, like it was all too big for your body, and I cried. You started crying for yourself as you decomposed and that was it, the moment I loved you.

10.   The Carpal Tunnel of Love

You are miserable and stunning. We sleep all weekend, force ourselves to say in bed because it is better than me, catching sight of you. In the morning, Oh My God, the sun rising behind your head, I'm full of an aching tunnel vision of you. At the table I'm shucking clams for dinner but then I'm still, knife tight in hand. If I broke you open, would I find pearls? I'd do if for just bones. You know how each part of you is so precious. I cannot help myself.

"I know, I know," you say. You don't know anything. The sun is imploding and you are still not saying "goodbye."

11.   Bang the Doldrums

Did you want a confession or a curse? This home is enough. This is all enough. That's what we say until it's night and we're not at home, we're on the sidewalk, not holding hands, trying to hail a cab. The driver asks where we want to go and we both say nothing, thinking without an answer can just ride endlessly, wandering the earth right up to the edge of it. Maybe we can live there next- maybe we'll watch the world end for the rest of our lives. You roll the windows down and breath in the rushing air as if you could hoard it all for yourself. Maybe you can. Please, suffocate the whole city.

12.   Fame < Infamy

I'm looking for redemption, not salvation. Your real name is "God's Gift" and it's too much for the moment. You're waiting for something, you are sweating in it. What do you want? What if I became holy. What if I sacrificed myself by hanging from noose or hook. Maybe then you'd kiss my feet, maybe then the world could begin again.

The grass would grow tall, into the sky and block out all our vision until there was only green. Maybe we surface together-

(but I doubt it, I doubt it)

13.   You're Crashing, But You're No Wave

What's worst about you is how little you hurt me. I can't work with a limp hand. It's like the edge of a storm that never comes. There's static in the air. It makes you stand on end. It makes me stand on the ceiling. What great things we can accomplish together. The girls are crying- the birds are screaming- You read the newspaper and I dance in circles. How are you not restless like me? How are you so perfect?

14. I've Got All This Ringing in My Ears and None on My Fingers

This is the truth: love comes from time. I have known you for such a long time. You know by now I hate you. I am always genuine in each of this things.

I'm in the car and the CD you bought me in highschool is playing. Funny how a thing can last. I sing along with the wrong lyrics. You're in the passenger seat and it's so dark. The cars are rushing by, and the light of the lamp posts look fat and painful from where they hover over us, flying. I consider turning into the wrong lane. You are here to to match. But you are curled up- you are silent and collapsed.

Sing? You are already bleeding. Sing? The song skips. The cars pass. Sing? The song skips. Sing? The cars come. Would you like to be buried here? If I swerved, would you only disappear? I never could hold you. Sing? The song skips- Sing? The cars around us flicker- are we skipping? Are you singing? Tell me, what is the worst thing I could do to you?

I hold your hand. Oh, love, no one wants to hurt you.

How could I ever—

Now press repeat

Albuquerque's Premier Bowling Center
AUGUST EDWARDS

It's all smoke stain yellow peeling paint
or wood and gleaming; sweaty bald heads.
Cold cokes in the machine, flat for months,
shoes splitting seams like that one couch we know
the cha-cha of triple-knotted feathered laces.
Beer-fingerprinted pink marble stratosphere
my ball careens to the edge of its Earth
like if *leaving* had a turbo booster.
Grease clutches the assist; it's out of my hands.
How can it feel so good to tear things down?
Pins in tens clatter all the way through the abyss
I guess they always come back up, though.
I can't afford to not knock them over.
Thank God and all His bumpers. It's a spare.

Underburning: Prepare an Era

BONNIE BEE

Autumn. An ancient archway of yellow leaves and pale tree trunks, a quiet sidewalk as the neighbors bow their heads in church. The city's breath kicks up, cool and wet, and it smells like someplace I used to know.

We will meet, I remember whispering into the night, into Oberon's ear as rain fell outside in a gentle song, and there we may rehearse most obscenely and courageously.

Two backpacks. Two tickets. I stand on the Nostrand platform, watching A-trains fly by on their tracks, Manhattan-bound. My heart beats patient and strong in my chest, because I'm waiting for Far Rockaway.

Every five to fifteen years, fire regenerates the forest and cleanses the understory of potential hazardous fuels.

Coffee and pretzels, coffee and cookies, an undying wish for laxatives and sleeping pills. I will be with thee anon, I write to Oberon while my hands shake, while I sit in the sky, not believing my own words, not even as my heart pounds, impatient and strong.

Fire plays an important and critical role in influencing vegetation and the lifecycle of trees and plant communities.

The welcome zone sits right outside those frosted glass doors, and it sounds unnatural, more like a place where people go to meet an end than to greet family, and it's a place where I'm not sure I belong

I stand in a room that smells like piss and every mirror is looking at me, saying, gentle Robin, go thou yon, for you must now to Oberon

Hands shaking as the door is pushed open—by my hand? By some great and helpful force, and I see a good familiar creature, but bigger, kinder.

Oberon's wide eyes and his simple nod, and all I can do is push forward until I collide with his frame, two backpacks dropping to the floor, one ticket gone, arms wrapping around a body that is stronger than before

Welcome, good Robin, he says, rough sandpaper voice, and we begin to move, to float, through sliding doors and into the sun-drenched prairie, and Oberon bends like a willow to kiss me, and push my mouth into his rough sandpaper face, where he tastes the same.

Controlled fires are used in order to improve forest health, and reduce large wildfires.

Many species are dependent on fire.

Now, my Robin; wake you, my sweet queen, Oberon mumbles onto the flat space behind my ear, and I stir, shifting into his broad warmth, his arms folding over me, and I feel safe there. Lips on the back of my neck, my ass against the length of his cock, and I bow my head.

Throughout time, wildfires ignite and burn naturally through the forest; they cause fast nutrient recycling.

A tongue on me in the darkness of our room, flat and wet, hands pushing my thighs open like a bible, my back arching, fingers gripping his hair, and then I'm shuddering under his attention, gasping and squeezing my legs around his shoulders

The Hunter's Moon hangs on a hook outside our window, painting blue grass grey as I ride, baring my teeth at Oberon in fierce desire as he stares up at me with blasted vision, my hand pressed down on his chest, the frantic beat of his heart.

The wildest hath not such a heart as you, he mutters, and rocks himself up into my body, brushing along the depth of me.

Come, my lord, I whisper against his cheek, shoving my hips back with purpose, the damp sound of our bodies colliding, a crack of sharp pleasure out of his mouth as he thrusts deep, fingernails digging into my skin, the delicate pulse of his cock inside me as he shudders my name.

Following a wildfire, an abundant supply of nutrients helps new seedlings, brush, and grasses to grow quickly and become established.

This one has seen more devils than vast Hell can hold, I think, clutching Oberon's head while he remembers, as his hot breath gusts over my stomach, as he wraps himself around me, wailing his anguish into the deep night, sheets rucked up around us, a makeshift shelter from his desert.

Kestrels make lazy spirals in the sun-scraped sky, an endless flight in search of something as we walk hand-in-hand, and we remember.

Slowly decomposing materials release nutrients steadily into the soil. This continuous release helps to maintain growth over a long period of time.

There's a cathedral in the trees, branches curving upward, spider's webs catching the light as it pours through and spills onto the ground, splashing onto Oberon's face and shoulders as he holds warm rocks in his hands and turns them over like precious eggs, and my heart beats, strong and affectionate.

Silver splashes across the water as fish skim the surface, a brilliant white twist in the air as a crane pitches into flight.

I close my eyes and there's a child, the one that bled out into my jeans one thin and icy winter so long ago, but she stands there, little fingers tugging on the fabric of our shirts, wild auburn hair, bright eyes, and I wonder what we would have named her.

The sun and I both kiss his face, wetness gathering and spilling from the corners of our eyes as I smile, and we bow our heads, and this is what forgiveness feels like, my heart breaking to allow him back in, scales cracking and falling away like dust.

The forest needs both slow recycling, from decomposition, and fast recycling from fires.

It's dusk. We collect our branches and roots and share them for the first time, weave them into a basket near a lake, knowing we're going to fill it with fresh soil and seed, knowing there will be more

It's dusk and we're chasing away the shadowy monsters that look like us, and I kiss Oberon's temple, listening to the steady, strong, loving beat of my heart

And I know a place where the sandgrass blows, where wild hops and the velvet devil's tree grow, quite over-canopied with luscious love vine, with sweet musk cardinals and with blister pine.

The Birds

KYLIE AYN YOCKEY

The birds know I'm one of them—
they heard my mother cooing
at tiny flightless me
back in the nest.
Everywhere I walk
they watch me, wait
for me and squawk at me and
wonder
if I find the dice and prairie dog bones and abandoned engagement rings
they leave on my roost.
I wonder:
do they see
what I collect for them too?
The VHS tapes and sticks of eyeliner and shot glasses and many memories
I seed into the cornfields
back home?
I stand up on my cross above the crops, spread my wings, know they won't be
scared.
They know me.

Marigolds

CRIS GALVEZ

The box arrived on the front porch in late October. There was no return address, but the box was marked with a priority mail sticker and covered in a thick layer of shiny, yellow tape. One of the corners was completely smashed in and the exposed cardboard edges were frayed. When Maisie first brought the box inside, it sat on the coffee table in the living room where she used it as a coaster for drinks, or as a footrest. When the holiday season rolled around, she wrapped the box in some shiny, silver tinsel and put her Christmas candles on top of it so it would match her home's festive decor. After celebrating New Year's, she put the decorations away before moving the box into the kitchen and setting it on the end of the dining room table where it sat quietly, collecting stacks of unopened mail.

It didn't occur to Maisie to open the box until the middle of January, when it began to snow inside her apartment. Thick, grey clouds swept across the ceiling like one massive, downy blanket. After two days of lingering in the air, heavy and pregnant, the clouds finally burst with big, fat flakes. They whirled down, sticking to the carpet in sticky clumps and Maisie had to sleep bundled up in her scarf, and hat, and poofy winter coat to keep warm when the temperature dropped at night. It didn't matter where she slept because the snow followed her throughout the apartment, although it never followed her into the dining room. Maisie had assumed the snow wasn't sticking in the dining room because there wasn't any carpet. To her surprise, when she walked into the kitchen, Maisie found a fresh blanket of fresh snow, sparkling in the sunlight shining in through the window above the sink. So Maisie stood in her snow boots in the kitchen, making herself a cup of tea, and thinking—for the first time—about the box she'd never opened. By this point, it was buried under several large piles of dusty envelopes and magazines, untouched by snow. She glanced over her shoulder at the box as the kettle on the stove puffed clouds of steam into the air.

Maisie's older sister, Ursula, called around 1pm. When the phone rang, Maisie was sitting at the dining room table, a mug of untouched, cold tea in her hands. She'd been staring at the box on the other end of the table all morning, hoping it would vanish if she stared at it long enough. The box had spent nearly three months in her apartment, and it was only now that it was drawing her attention. There was no return address and Maisie wondered how she'd rationalized taking a box without a return address inside her house when anthrax was being shipped through the mail—not that she was important enough to have anthrax sent to her through the mail, but the box could possibly be filled with anthrax. Maisie's stomach twisted into a pretzel. She picked up the phone, convincing herself that if the box were full of anthrax, she probably would have fallen ill already.

Maisie took a deep breath and answered the phone. "Hello?"

"How have you been, Maisie?" Ursula asked. "It's been a while. Mom is starting to worry about you."

Maisie ran her hand along the back of her neck, fingers searching for the mole she'd been picking for years.

"Yeah," Maisie said, glancing up at the box on the table as she dug her fingers against the mole's scabby rim. "Sorry."

"Any chance you'd be able to swing by my house sometime later this week?" Ursula asked, her voice quavering. Maisie's eyes were still fixated on the box. The mail on top of the box was shifting and tumbling onto the table's surface, as if an invisible hand was pushing it.

"No," Maisie said, wedging her nail under the scab. "I mean, I would love to, but I just can't this week."

There was a long pause between them and Maisie knew Ursula was expecting her to say something else—or maybe apologize.

"Maisie, listen, I know you're still upset."

Maisie slide her nail under the rim of the mole and felt warm blood smear against the tip of her thumb as she wiggled her finger beneath the rim, wincing in spite of herself.

"But don't you—" Ursula hesitated. "I only mean to say, maybe it would help you feel better if—"

"Sula, just drop it, okay?" Maisie said. Suddenly, a loud PUFF made Maisie jump from her chair, knocking it over as she stumbled backwards, pressing herself back against the back door. The mail was scattered all over the table and the two flaps on the surface of the box were standing up upright in the air. After several seconds, they began to inch downward as gravity pulled at them.

"Maisie, please," Ursula whined. "I know this is hard for you, but it's been years now."

Maisie tore her eyes away from the box and glanced down at her footprints in the snow. It had been a few years, hadn't it? There was no reason to be this upset over a box of something. If there was anthrax in there, she'd be dead soon anyways—that was how anthrax worked, right? Right?

"Sula, I gotta go. Goodbye." Maisie hung up the phone.

The snow in the kitchen was cold. Maisie squatted, holding her phone in one hand, her back to the dining room table. In the reflection on the oven door, Maisie saw tiny wooden tendrils creeping up out of the open box. There wasn't any anthrax in the box—now she knew it was just a box that had been delivered to her apartment, maybe by mistake, but she was stuck with it now. It would have to stay sitting on her kitchen table, possibly forever.

"You shouldn't blame yourself, Maisie," Maisie heard Ursula whispering into her ear as the tendrils curled and twisted around each other, forming a scrawny, leaning trunk. "Maybe it just wasn't meant to be."

Maisie watched branches furl out from the trunk in every direction, dragging a tiny, grey onesie speckled with yellow and green ducks from the bottom of the box, littering the floor with packing peanuts. Maisie tore her eyes away from the reflection in the oven door and grabbed a handful of snow, jamming it against the back of her neck and held it there, squeezing her eyes shut, ignoring the icy burn clawing into her skin, stinging her mole. Each shiver running up her spine spread through her body and cleared the fuzz away from the images of those tiny ducks in the back of her mind.

"After all," Ursula continued from her place on the couch, running a hair brush through her own daughter's stringy, toddler curls. "He wouldn't have been right in the head. Now you don't have to deal with that."

Maisie's hand slipped from her neck, leaving the snow to melt on her skin, the tree branches sprouting bunches of fern-like leaves. Fluffy, crinkled, yellow and orange marigold blossoms popped out from stems at the end of the branches. The little onesie hung limply, tangled in the tree's upper-most branches, marigolds blooming through the open zipper in front and poking through the sleeves.

"And I'm sure, in time, you'll try again and forget all about this one," Ursula's voice was gentle as she put the brush down and pulled her daughter onto her lap.

It hadn't been years. It had been one year—just a year since she'd folded that stupid onesie, placed it in a box, and filled that box with packing peanuts, because that was all that was left of him. Maisie pulled her knees up to her chest and hugged them as the snow on her neck slipped down the back of her shirt in a soupy slush. Behind her, marigolds continued to spiral upwards through the branches, abandoning their stems, floating and crawling towards the onesie. They blossomed out of the fabric itself, petals chewing through the zipper and tiny plastic pads on the bottom of the feet, but still Maisie refused to turn around. Instead, she opened her eyes and watched through the reflection in the oven door as the Marigold's stuffed themselves inside the onesie in a panicked frenzy. And, in the slightly blurred reflection, Maisie thought she saw the seam along the onesie's side tearing open with tinges of orange and gold.

"Everything happens for a reason, Maisie," Ursula whispered, wrapping an arm around Maisie and pulling her into a side embrace. "Please try to cheer up."

"No!" Maisie cried as she threw herself at the oven door. "No, no, stop it! Stop!" she cried, pounding her fists against the reflection.

Shadow

KYLIE AYN YOCKEY

A child's room is basked in light—

      twinkling galactic mobile over baby-soft bed,

      glow-in-the-dark stars stuck to crown molding,

      sunshine night-light kissing the edge of a vined, white crib.

A mother carries toys, plush pillows, lullabies on her breath.

      In socked toes she dances with, coos at, whispers love to an unworn teddy bear.

A father, standing in the doorway, sheds his composure,

      lets it slip from his eyes down his face,

      watching his wife—

She looks like midnight: haunted, dressed in black, silent as the grave.

Family Portrait

LINDSEY TOWNSEND

I was not in it. A picture was taken not long after I left town for my first year of college. Cousins were visiting, outside on a sunny day, standing on my grandmother's porch—a place so familiar to me that I can smell it: the sturdy, sheltered deck hidden in a quiet little part of a pine tree town, looking over a well-worked garden, echoing memories through sandstone canyons. The porch itself was relatively new, but how many times through the years had I entered that beat up white door and, no doubt, let it slam behind me. They stood in front of it in a close group, the way a family should, with happy expressions on well-known faces. Even the 3-year-old was smiling—my grandma holding her impatient hand. My other sister had on a radiant grin, the one she always wore. My grandpa was standing behind my mom, who was wearing pink. *How ironic,* I thought. And barely noticed what was missing; barely noticed how her chest laid flat under her shirt—a sight I hadn't seen in person yet. Tonight my mind was not in what was missing, but in memories of many failed attempts at making homemade pizza. In memories of mac and cheese still warm in the dish, and cinnamon oven-toast on lazy weekend mornings. In memories of ketchup with seemingly everything on a small, Mickey Mouse plate. Tonight what was missing did not matter as much as what was not. My uncomfortable desk chair pulled up to my uncomfortable desk, the family portrait hanging on the wall by my lamp. My mother's kind, accepting face looking over me as I did my work, just like it always had. She watched me with that look I knew so well.

And though I was sitting in an unfamiliar dorm room eight hours away, and things were harder than ever—with the cancer, and the depression, and the guilt, and the pain—she was still in the picture.

Blueshift
BONNIE BEE

It's the night before Christmas, and I'm telling my father I want to move in with my mother.

A snowstorm, a silence, an upside down smile, and I'm uninformed that he's 39 and angry about his impending 40, weary in the wake of my continual adolescence.

The past three years have been romantically rewarding for my father. As a man who needs a woman to help him raise his daughter, he's been working hard to find a match. I can't remember how many dates, but he garnered a handful of serious relationships through this time, outside of the holy crusades he endured with my mother.

We have Christmas lights—*Christmas* lights, not holiday lights. We're living in Texas, "holiday lights" are for...*liberals*. They twinkle and wink and blink, dance and prance, and make merry all over the place for our Lord Jesus (who was not born in December) (but here we are), and those blinking, winking lights are so vexing in that cumbersome instant, when I have popcorn between my teeth. In that moment when my father won't look at me.

Now, Bonnie, dear, you do know your mother is terrible, he says. Pine wood in the fireplace from faraway misty mountains, and *crackle-pop* goes the warm, crispy sap.

Jane was my father's rebound, fresh off the marriage, and she's my favorite. Her family had been a long-term friend of ours until her husband, Ralph, ran off with a 19-year-old college sophomore, leaving Jane to deal with their three children until the divorce was final.

She was tall and pear-shaped, her laugh was exquisite, and she was kind. I caught them in a tongue-wrestling match behind my father's truck one chilly night in September after they sent me into the grocery store for milk. I wanted her to be my mother.

Dad, I say, and I have popcorn between my teeth, and in my braces— which is very uncomfortable. Uncomfortable like the way he won't look at me. Uncomfortable like a first kiss.

Now dear, you know she's a crazy, he says. You do remember when she came home and begged me to take her back, she came into the house, curled up on the bed, cried into a pillow like a child? Remember when I sent her away? That's because she's a crazy.

I do remember that. I also remember the afternoon they rushed off to the hospital and my sister watched over me while they were gone. That night, when they came home in a whisper, my mother wouldn't look up from her feet when she told us that she lost the baby.

I remember the way they used to hold each other and kiss in the surf when we would take family trips to Corpus Christi beach, their young, tan bodies like demigods as they pressed into one another. They would help us build elaborate sand castles with moats and towers, and show us how to safely feed the seagulls—until mom's finger was sliced open on a beak.

Brenda's next on the list. Not on my list of favorites, but in timeline, and she also held out the longest. A dating website brought them together: he, a survivor of my mother, and her, a survivor of brain surgery. She was uncomfortable with how I liked to walk around in my bra, and I was uncomfortable with how my father would touch the small of her back, right above her ass, to guide her as she walked.

One night of sugar-fueled silliness in the family mobile home brought me and her 15-year-old sister together. Her name was Natasha. Lingerie was our favorite topic through giggles and blushing, and then I touched her waist like a only a boy should, and she kissed me hard and wet. We never talked about it again, or much else. I wanted to be good, and at the same time I love to be wanted, and I wanted her.

Rumpled mobile home bed sheets were explained away with stories of late afternoon naps and rough-housing, because were were tomboys, after all, and being a tomboy is so convenient. It's much easier to hide from the brimstone my father spits when I show him that I can also be his son.

Two months later, my dad and Brenda separated. Brenda and Natasha's brother had died of AIDS in a hospital, refusing to accept the Lord Jesus into his life every step of the way. Now Bonnie, you know AIDS is a sin, he told me the morning of the funeral. It's gay people cancer.

The pink that bloomed on my cheek about the size of my father's hand from that one summer afternoon when my anger boiled over, and he was seeking to keep control. He answered a lot of questions in that instant with the back of his hand, and I wondered if anyone else knew what that felt like. I wondered if the women he brought home might know something about that.

Now he's alone, raising a daughter who he wants to be a son, who he wants to be good, and I just want to be with my mother.

And I could hear him say: You know Bonnie is a terrible daughter. You do remember when she came back here and begged me to take her back, she came into the house, curled up on my bed, cried into a pillow like a child?

Christmas lights, green and blue and white, twinkling and blinking and torturing me, existential dread of what does it all mean, and the popcorn is still stuck between my teeth

And everything is fine

There was the one lady whose name I don't remember, the one he brought home after just a few weeks of dating to watch Braveheart with us, who only lasted a solitary night after she said…curse words…in front of his 14-year-old daughter. She was my second favorite, and I wish I could remember her name as I'm sitting on the couch, staring at my father, who's staring at the tree.

And in this moment I'm sure my dad was having all the premarital sex he was trying to contain in me, and I've decided that's because you only have to wait 'til marriage the first time, see, that's the loophole.

My father says: Now dear, you can never come back if you leave. Crackle-pop goes something in my chest.

But everything is fine. Even if it feels like brain surgery. Just a girl going through puberty, wondering if she's going to be a crazy, too. Wondering if she'll be a survivor, or a problem. Wondering why she wasn't born a boy, or good, or why she doesn't believe in god.

It's New Year's Eve, and I'm moving in with my mother.

He doesn't look at me. Just closes up the house, and leaves the garage door open until I'm out.

There are only a few discarded Christmas trees out on the curb in our cul de sac from the Scrooges who are just glad the holiday is over, and I put the last box into the back of my mother's truck. I never got the packages that were under the tree, the ones with my name on them.

But everything is just fine. Everything is just. Everything is, what it is, and I wish I was good, and I wish I was a boy, and I wish that he would look at me just one more time.

Nest
BRIANNA NEUMANN

When can I stop thinking about
this, stop blaming everything on this?
This single night, these nine long days,
these seventeen or fifty-seven years?
How can I know the egg of this,
this creature who has outgrown its nest?

He is a late-night ER psychiatrist, calling.
Coughing and callous, he asks, *has your mother*
done this before? Did she show signs, or
did she have a weapon? Is this my ancestry—
is this who we are? Are our limbs twisted
in twigs and brambles, wicked thistles?
Can't we pluck ourselves from the nettles?

My family is an animal, its pelt rank, tangled.
I can see its yellow eyes, as my grandma says
she'd been that way forever, as if my mother

has her own clustered clumps of DNA. Did they
think to help, to try to stop it? We pass the blame,
hold its fuzzy head to our chests, play a game,
to see who hates it best. I go home,
prize in hand, burrs burdened. How can I

let this go, drop and abandon
this feral thing that was handed down to me?

In June
KYLIE AYN YOCKEY

Summer child, born in
the heat and starshine, do you
see your own halo?

A One-Sided Conversation with the Cosmos in My Mother's Garden

LINDSEY TOWNSEND

The pink flowers in my mother's garden gaze up at me—tissue paper petals attached to soft, feathered greens. Scattered in the flower bed, I wonder of their namesake. How do these resemble stars? The Cosmos spread out above me, so vast, so complex, so... breathtaking compared to the tiny flowers in front of me. Each flower with its eight pink rays pointing out from a yellow middle. They fill the tired bed full to bursting, as my curiosity grows. These cosmos, unlike The Cosmos, so rooted and limited and humble. Are these flowers also ever expanding? Explosive? Made of light? Capable of extreme darkness?

I imagine an eruption of petals and a blinding light surrounding me in a fury of possibility.

Sol
KYLIE AYN YOCKEY

I worry that you feel like an asteroid
Like a rock revolving in a planet's rings—
Allow me to enlighten on astronomy:
You are a constellation, stars, a sun
The center of ellipses

Definition
BRIANNA NEUMANN

1. FIREARM

A pistol, rifle, machine gun, grenade,
or the key to a closed apartment
that I wish I still lived in, sometimes.
A weapon of some destruction, however
sweet and shiny and soft-eyed,
however twisted, ridged, grifted,
however small your feet became
when I nestled them in my lap
at the end of an endless rotted day.
A stretch between bullet and forehead,
a cocking unlocking motion.

2. PIGMENT

A coloring substance or matter, or
splatter of acrylic on kitchen floor.
You painted every place in our home,
and I scraped flakes of shades

from every scrunch and rented surface.
A mark left by dye, or bile,
long-hung and searching for white,
and I was discolored, sprayed on
by you and your deft, solid hands.
A fade that happens rosy, slowly,
so I can ascertain the difference
only after staggered weeks of waiting.

3. COMBUSTIBLE
or, capable of burning.
I am capable of burning.
But more importantly, I am capable
of deconstructing, of mismanaging
your fragile, fractured, bird-legged self.
Capable, of spontaneously sourcing
into smoke, of disarranging my atoms
and unbuilding. You wish you were
something seething hot and nothing,
something that crackles heart red,
ashy orange, pigments, exploding —
who knows, if you and I are firewood.

Cadaver
JUDITH RIPLEY

You scratched your initials into my flesh
like how teenage lovers carve theirs into the bark of a tree.
Except there was no plus sign, or heart, or promise of *4 Ever*.
There was music playing from the speaker in your living room,
our clothes were scattered on the floor,
a loose grip on my neck, and a hand between your thighs.
You were amazed with the way I squealed
like a pig being slaughtered when your nails dug in
and dragged them down my skin
from my collarbones and across my chest.
You giggled and said:
It looks like you had an autopsy.
I laughed along with you and proceeded to run
my hands through your hair, bringing your face closer to mine
so I could bite your neck and make you cry out
like I had found the Holy Grail of erogenous zones.
But once I learned your weaknesses
and used them to make you writhe underneath me,

you used your sweet talk, your lips, and your strength
to push me back into a
corner from which I could not escape.
I was not the one in control.
You made sure I understood that
and although I wanted to, I did not argue.
You kept retracing over the marks you left,
the scratches on my shoulder blades and the base
of my spine, the bite marks on my biceps, neck, and thighs.
My body was your cadaver,
to touch and tear to pieces, and I let you use me,
wholeheartedly,
because I liked it.
The adrenaline and hormones raged through my body,
making me feel helpless
yet invincible. Fragile yet
unbreakable. You pressed and squeezed my sides
like you were trying to crack my ribcage;
you wanted my bones to snap in half
like breaking a pencil. I brought your hand to my neck,
but never told you how badly I wanted you
to make me stop breathing.
I wanted to fade away into blackness
and let my body lay limp across your lap,
so you could do whatever you wanted to me
without my screams waking up the neighbors.

4 a.m., a Tuesday, and it is Raining
SCHUYLER HALL GILMORE

I answer on the fifth ring—
listen to your broken-record-pleading,

let you tell me you want me, that you're
sorry, but you're not sorry, but you want to be

all right. *Give me something.* Tell me you
love me more,

and I'll love you a little less for it.

Devour

KYLIE AYN YOCKEY

I pull her apart,
skin from slippery tendons.
My teeth suck out her
dark liver and I
tongue the empty space
between her bones—
This body is my rightful feast
and I will clean every slurp
of marrow out for all it is worth,
and then lick my fingers like
I enjoyed it.
She will be buried
in oozing tin foil,
because I am too chicken
to crush her
pieces down the sink.

The Tin Girl

JUDITH RIPLEY

With my chest, hollow and made of tin, I wield a rusty axe over my shoulder, and hold your tail between my metal fingers as we walk together down the yellow stone path. The trees throw their apples at us, instigating a fight, but they forget that you, my dear, are the Queen of the Forest. And that I was once a woodsman, who with one whack of my axe can silence their splintery threats if they continue to bruise the precious flesh hidden beneath your golden fur. Your cowardice shows when the flying monkeys perch themselves in the branches above our heads, watching us like vultures, your intimidating façade of courage starts to crack and your roars turn into whimpers and whines. But as soon as they start to point and laugh at my rusty metal joints and the clang of my cold armor, you puff out your chest and bare your teeth, sending them soaring back to the sky. My lioness, I swear to the stars that I feel the sparks from the wires trying to start the part of me that is missing, all because you protect me from anyone who looks at me as though I am nothing but walking, talking scrap metal. I wish I could do a better job at returning the favor. Next time someone—whether they be a tree or a monkey—tries to say you are less than a lion, I won't hesitate to use my axe and make it known that I will defend you at all costs. That despite my literal lack of a beating organ in my tin chest, the love I have for you is what keeps me alive and walking.

The Lioness

JUDITH RIPLEY

The trees, the trees revolt against me, throwing their apples at my metal body as I walk among them. Instead of an axe on my shoulder, I carry a coiled rope. The weight of it almost as heavy as my heart—if I had one. The trees, the trees won't tell me to stop. They won't tell me to go back home. When the rope is tied securely to one of their branches, they will tell me I was meant to be nothing but a wind chime. I stand upon a stump, the remains of a victim from when I was a woodsman. Now, I am just talking scrap metal, a heartless heartbreaker, and the trees laugh at my misery. They encourage me to cry, cry until my joints begin to rust and my wires begin to short-circuit. Suddenly there's a roar, a roar so deafening that stops me in my tracks, the rope resting in my metal palms. This roar is not one of intimidation. Its intention is not to scare the bark off their trunks and shake their leaves. It is one of complete and total anguish, a fierce reminder of how much I had hurt your lion pride. I called you a coward and a fraud, and you snarled and told me I was heartless and selfish. The phantom pains in my chest lasted for days, and today they are the most severe they have been. I sigh, and tighten the knot of the rope around my neck, the trees watching with sinister smiles. I feel a force push against my back and I lose my balance on the stump beneath my feet. The sound of the trees cheering and laughing at my metal body slowly fades as I flail. I see your shadow, from the depths of the green forest. A roar rings out as I hang.

Saudade
SCHUYLER HALL GILMORE

I painted for you, a canvas of stars, silent
reminders, broken little things—

and their forged alabaster gaze left me
consumed and daunted by a lackluster love.

For days, I fought the flood—

blackened out each little leading light, until
there was nothing left but the grief and

a starless sky.

Nothing's Gonna Change My World
ZOE BAILLARGEON

1.

It seems to be my lot in life that when loss comes calling, I am geographically unavailable to answer the door.

"Sorry, no one's home!"

I don't mean to imply that because I am far away, loss passes me by. Leaves a scribbled note, shoved under the door: "Will try back later." Jiggles the doorknob. Realizes it has the wrong house and retreats down the driveway.

I've simply just not been home for when loss shows up unexpectedly. And loss is a rude houseguest, so it lets itself in regardless of my presence. Sifts through my mail. Helps itself to whatever's in the fridge. Runs its finger over everything, swabbing for dust.

And eight thousand miles away, I feel the intruder in my home, in my bones, and shiver.

2.

My new home has mountains on one side and an ocean on the other. At the top there is heat and sand, at the bottom a raging sea. The borders are stretched thin, like many other things here as well: budgets, patience, distance.

We live in the illusion the world cannot touch us for our mountains, our sea, our sand, our infallible nature. Geographic factors affect an insular mindset.

Protected by our topographical guardians, we sit at our tables, drinking tea and watching the rest of the world spin by -- clay figurines in a snow globe. Our fixed points are within our four walls. What happens in the far, far north, has no effect on us, for we are in the south. What happens in the far, far south, has no effect on us, for we are not that far south. Bad politics? War? The country has suffered plenty, and could do it again. Nothing can touch us.

But change always comes, like wind and water, forcing a path.

3.

The world turns slower for me, watching from my sliver of land. Things that once seemed so essential have turned opaque, lost that thrum of urgency.

Everything in the world moves. Wind, water, sand, people. Flight patterns. Tectonic plates. But here, I'm out of the flow. Actions and consequences can only marginally touch me. Life swirls around me—a rock in a stream.

It's this sensation that makes me feel that I can still pick up the phone, dial the number, and she'll still pick up. He'll still pick up. The places I knew will be just as I left them last.

The idea that nothing changes simply because you cannot bear witness to it.

4.

Staying a time zone ahead of bad news doesn't stop it. Maybe delays it a little. It shows up at the airport, sallow-faced, reeking of filtered air. It stumbles from a silver tube into the light, blinking. Then it goes to your door and punches you in the face.

"Thanks for forgetting to pick me up at the airport, asshole."

"I didn't even know to be expecting you."

"Yeah, well, I'm here now. Where's my room?"

5.

Since it seems to be my lot in life to be away when loss comes calling, there is a delayed reckoning. A five-second delay, but amplified by eight thousand miles and the Earth's spin and gravitational pull and fluctuating time zones.

Emotional jet lag.

What's been lost — people, places, memories — exist in an alternate dimension. Because I'm not there for their physical absence, they persist.

They're still alive in the cellular dead zone where, because I cannot receive the call, she's still in a coma.

Because they're five hours behind, he can still nonchalantly wander through the cat door and we can laugh at how worried we were. I protect myself by being in the future.

Because there are so many miles between us, so many other people living out their lives, so many variables keeping the world turning, he could not fall.

Because I don't want to believe it, the classrooms still fill up in the morning and empty at night. The night guard still ignores the smell of weed from dorm windows. There is still laughter, tears, jokes. The place where I took root, blown in by the wind, can be that for others.

But the breathing still stops. The machines still turn off. The papers are still signed. The pallbearers still bear. Regardless of whether I'm there or not.

They're gone, but they're still there until I go back, when the illusion crumbles like clay.

6.

There is no actual map for navigating loss.

There are guideposts, legends in the margins, but no mile markers between them, no sense of distance. There are sentries — "This way for your denial phase, pit stop here for rage, go now, there won't be another stop until coping with your own mortality" — but no connecting paths.

You're meant to stumble the same dark path everyone on Earth stumbles down at one point or another, hands colliding in the dark —"Whoops, sorry, didn't see you there" —and keep on stumbling. Airplanes in the night. Hoping we don't collide and take everyone down with us.

7.

At any given moment of any given day, my life exists within the radius of 33° S, 71° W, give or take about a hundred kilometers.

That has been my fixed point, and the lines that define my world, imposing depth, context, meaning, extend outward.

From my tiny red house by the sea, I can triangulate my world.

8,000 miles to the home they no longer occupy. The now re-inhabited nursing home apartment.

8,692 miles to the house I can no longer go home to. The dormitories and classrooms left empty. The lost home.

Viewed that far away, the image loses definition. Blurs. The fixed lines of my world snap free, waving in the breeze like loose threads from a spiderweb.

I cope in my own way.

I know eventually, I need to go home. Leave the shelter of the mountains and ocean. Span those eight thousand miles. Be back where I began.

I need to visit those graves.

And when I do, the world will realign. The lines snap into place.

I will be broken and whole.

And the way will be a little bit clearer for next time...

First
JOSE ARAGUZ

—and then the sun looked down upon the earth, took in how countless and unending life here seemed, saw in it something of the universe, at least what he knew of it, boundless and crowded, only what he saw was a thing that held nothing as bright as he was, nothing that aspired to take his place, nothing even to take a place beside him, and he continued in his thoughts, taking note of everything in regards to what he could not see, trying to block out his reflection which is all he saw—on the water, on the leaves—his thoughts multiplying and emptying him until he looked at the ground and saw shapes, dark, no light in them, a whole world that was not a world but a passing feeling that moved as he moved. The first shadows looked back at the sun—

Dying for the End, Part One
KYLIE AYN YOCKEY

I'm dying for the end of the world
      when no mass nor matter will matter
      in the end

for the earth to sheath me in locust wings
      a shell   chrysalis tomb
This body will rot
      until I'm merely moss on the aged steel
      bones of cityscapes

My soft green skin won't know the wars   the hunger
      will photosynthesize   sustain
I'll want for nothing but my own breath   the north star   and
      continued catastrophe

Dying for the End, Part Two
KYLIE AYN YOCKEY

I'm dying for the end of the world. Ever since the steel cityscapes crumbled under their own weight, deleting millions of people with each falling skyscraper, I've been trapped under masses of broken metal matter. It's like a cracked ribcage of wires, screens, and gears, entombing me half-in-half-out of what was once the hospital I spent my soft human life in.

I was dying before we crashed and burned. My cells were rotting from the inside out, plaguing my fleshy shell. *Let us implant you,* the doctors and technicians and forward-thinkers begged, *fill you with our wires and gears, stop your body's war on you.* They didn't understand my resistance, why I still wanted to be organic in a world where we could starve ourselves of grain and milk, full-bellied on data and oil and be ever preserved. I can admit that I am a creature of science, born by cause-and-effect and powered by atoms regenerating – but I am also a believer in alchemy, and I know my particles were once stardust, magic of the universe. My possessive nature about my body is because I only possess this body; it belongs to nature.

So they and them and all logged their brains onto the main circuit's collective subconscious, replacing bones with ceramic and curing all iron deficiencies. People were living forever. Their synthetic flesh vessels fought more wars, conquered more and more until everyone and their mother was forty pounds heavier with motherboards. I was insignificant enough to slip through the screenings, barely a blip on the radar, so I alone kept dying.

But then the buildings force-quit. For all the intellect, for all the shared intelligence, no one accounted for gravity. The physical world couldn't keep up anymore, so it all fell down. Everyone short-circuited, buzzing and frying as one under the rubble. I'm the single consciousness left, lying in a damaged glass and concrete chrysalis.

My body is already starting to decompose. My internal clock says it's been many days, but I rejected the timepiece implant so I don't really know. The sun has risen and moon waned over the open ceiling, replacing the nurse-operated fluorescent fixtures. Festering since birth, my insides are already ready for carrion status, and my skin is starting to grow moss. Under the unending eye of the North Star above, the green is photosynthesizing, sustaining my breath. Outside is continued catastrophe; I can hear the thunder of more cities deteriorating, brightening up sections of my little bit of sky with lightning from the ground up. As the solitary person who loved the earth un-upgraded, I can't say I mind that nature is taking the world back.

It is possible that the minds of people have just been transferred to satellites, uploaded above the clouds, but I like to think that when I finally die like the rest of the man-made things, then while my body will decay back into the earth, my mind will be made up into the atmosphere, return to the cosmos.

Remembrance
IVY STOVER

You crawl into my lap,
lay your cheek against my shoulder,
press your nose to my pulse point,
"We're going to die."

Warm tears slide down my breast,
my arms settle around your hips.
There are no sirens or screams,
just a single bomb slipping through the clouds
like a blanket of ash.

Your hands clutch at my shirt,
nails tearing through the fabric
and into my skin.
I don't flinch.

The bomb is closer now.
I press you tighter to my chest,

align my fingers with the notches
in your spine.
"I don't want to be forgotten."

Your heart beats against my ribs,
my breath drifts across your ear—
the bomb touches down.

The corpses of Pompeii know each other's names.

Permian
MADELEINE SARDINA

I.   Earth's core is too old to be known by anyone. She has pulsed for 4.5 billion years, hot and molten. In Russia, scientists—men—tried to dig through to the center, through the permafrozen crust, first. They punched a nine-inch wide hole deep into the hardened soil, looking for oozing magma and evidence of Earth's heart. They broke her skin, shoved hands and heads inside that narrow hole and clawed up fragments of granite. But those Archean layers were hard and dark, built by the pummeling Earth took in her youth. Frostbite stung the flesh of those frozen men and the bubbling rage of Earth boiled their instruments, but still they dug. The hole sobbed up mud bubbling with instability: chaos and hydrogen. The scientists stood at the gash they had plowed into Earth's skin and forced more tools down deeper still. They searched for the hot glow of magma. They searched for basalt and the water that whispered songs of old life. Their bones cracked and collapsed before they breached the crust.

II.   Two hundred and fifty million years ago, Earth tried to destroy herself. She gouged her iron and nickel skin with meteors, still slinging through space from the center of the universe. The holes left by those space stones spewed up lava and sulfuric fumes made from long-dead bodies. Earth took great, toxic breaths and held them tight in her core until smoke oozed from every pore. Every living thing absorbed Earth's putrid breath. Gray clouds of death clogged the sky, drowning the great lizards, the great cold-blooded beasts, in shadow. Their bodies collapsed beneath the weight of Earth's suicide. The oceans, birthplace of her children, boiled with poison. Her skin turned coal-black and red and what remained alive hid in the crevices of the scaled skin of her suffocated children.

III. I wonder if the thing that made Earth plucked her from some cosmic tree. If he or they or it plucked two, bit into the first and found it hard and bitter. If they tossed the second, our unripe planet, into empty space and left her to rot. I wonder if they forgot rotten things are where life starts. Before that life, in the wee morning hours of the Big Bang, came heat. Stardust, still universe dust then, fused together by the weight of everything around it. Our earth, like our sun and neighbor planets, was born from combustion. The vacuum of space moved slower by every second but then, still young and full of energy, it flowed quickly over itself. It built a cosmos in that constant, burning shift and when it finally cooled and crusted over, we emerged from the forge.

Ossuary
CHANTELLE MITCHELL

Sandstone cathedrals, towering cinnamon mounds jutting up into the sky on an otherwise unassuming and vastly empty dirt plane. A creamy monolith with its eye on me. The slithering of desert snakes and centuries-old bones rattling just inches underground where they've shifted up and up throughout the years, slowly creeping in search of calcium-rich sisters. It's hot, but the hairs raise on my arms and neck like texture tattoos: dry leaves etched onto my forearms, a glyph of goosebumps on my wrist. Everyone says the desert is lonely but that's just because they forget their kin in the sand who were buried and forgotten and are rotting with scorpion tails and coyote teeth.

The sun is at its peak and so is the strumming in my chest. It's Monday. I should be in my cubicle coffin, dead with eyes open after two cups of coffee, holding a bouquet of invoices. Instead I'm using my bare fingers to dig into the red sand, looking for my mothers and brothers and children. I don't have permission to enter the bone city beneath me, but I'll force my way in.

I miss my sister. I know she's at work now, doing what she loves, existing in a space where people have reason to exist – far away from me. I'm tired of looking for a purpose. Instead I'll become one.

The toughness of the bone can be partially attributed to things called "sacrificial bonds"; right there in the collagen, sparing themselves to make the bone stronger—breaking apart and sucking in external energy that would otherwise cause a crack. Like a mother jumping in front of a bullet for her child, or an older brother breaking your fall when you try standing on a chair to reach the top shelf.

Scarlett used to take the blame for me when something caught fire, when I was too busy experimenting with life to notice everything charred behind me. She's only two years older than me, but already her divine armor has chinks in it. She took responsibility for the cigarettes our mother found in my coat pocket when I was fifteen. On nights when the roaring insults upstairs were louder than the blaring cartoon dog on the television, she covered for me when I crept out and hid in the shed. When our father's wrist snapped, his palm cracking across my cheek, she wound her fingers around his neck like it was Play-Doh. And when, in an anger-induced struggle, I left scars on her face where I scratched my nails deep into her cheek, she made up an excuse about falling into some bushes while she was trying to sneak out, successfully keeping our parents' critical gaze only on herself. I watched her disinfect the cuts with a sad smile on her face, her love in every drop of red growing slowly, spreading like wild vines in the lines of the damp paper towels.

She's spent too much of her energy on me. In turn, I never got hurt, but I never grew either—a dry stump next to her sturdy ash tree. She's too used to sacrifice; it made her into a desirable friend, employee, partner, human being. She understands things I do not. She has goals and drive and plans. I don't know what I want except to be protected and comforted by her sacrificial bond again and again.

It used to be a team sport between the two of us, we learned what sacrifice was together. Giving things up to protect what was precious to us: skinny bodies, pretty faces, a quiet night at home with no screaming father.

My sister is beautiful in a way that taught me ugly things can still be precious. Her eyes are too far apart and her lips are so thin that they disappear into her teeth when she talks. But when the sun shines her freckles dance on her face, do a jovial two-step and foxtrot and glide over the bridge of her nose. In the sunlight she's beautiful.

One day in the summer when I was braiding her hair and we were humming together on the back porch, she told me she knew she was ugly.

"I'll have to work twice as hard, won't I? I don't have a charming smile or anything. That's how people get what they want."

"Eh. There are lots of idiots behind nice smiles," I said. "You're a genius, Scarlett."

I felt her as she gulped from a can of warm Dr. Pepper, my fingers at the nape of her neck as I weaved through her silk hair.

"I'm smart, but you're smart *and* pretty." She said this simply, without any bite. "I used to hate being the ugly sister."

I didn't try to correct her.

"What do you want to be, Cora? After high school." She looked back at me from the corner of her eye.

"I don't know?" I tied off the end of her hair. "I'll sound stupid if I say something like 'happy' or 'useful', right? I know you think that stuff's corny."

She laughed, her eyes scrunching up like wet paper. "As expected. I like that you're corny, though. My corny sister."

"My ugly sister."

She smiled back at me, a playful look bubbling in her premature crow's feet. "I think I want to be an osteologist or something. Bone science, you know?"

"You creep. Why?"

"You find out so much just from skeletons buried in the sand or in rubble or in caves: whole histories and families. Don't you think it would be kind of profound if my purpose in life was to figure out the purpose of life for those creatures whose bones we walk all over every day?"

"Profound. Or morbid." I felt the creases in my forehead deepen.

She lifted her arm in front of my face and traced the goosebumps on that were forming. "I'm getting excited just thinking about it."

I wanted to know what it felt like to get goosebumps in July, too.

When we were younger, the question was always, "What do you want to be?"
It slowly morphed into, "What's your major?" Cocooning and growing in a college
chrysalis, never ceasing to intimidate me. And then finally, "What do you do?" – the
supposed beautiful reveal, the emergence. I think I was too big boned to properly
develop as a pupa and I jumped into it all prematurely, without ever answering the
essential first question. *What do you want to be?*

I hate questions like that. What did my mother want to be? What did my
landlord want to be? What did the man who stands outside of McDonald's want
to be? I don't think they filled out their senior surveys in blood, don't think they
wrote *broke* or *anxious* or *homeless* as they were picking up their caps and gowns. I
surely didn't write *dead*.

Maybe I'll find answers from these bones. They died – so will I. I've decided
they're going to keep me company. I shovel the burning sand with my hands and
wince until my palms finally go numb and I can proceed without feeling. The
bodies living here in this tawny pool on the side of the highway probably don't even
belong to any of my ancestors, but I tell myself all humans are connected and keep
shoveling anyway.

I'm still digging as my sister's words ring through my head. My life's purpose?
To die, probably. Not in a suicidal way, but in a way that triggers rebirth and release
and resurrection in someone else: my sister, whose purpose is to explain the lives
of the dead while she stands in a lab all day. A nine to five sounds like torture, and
I've decided I'd rather be buried alive. I'll be useful to her; it'll be just like a part-
time job.

I keep digging. One fistful of sand for every year of college I had to go through.
One grain for every dollar of debt. One fried, shriveled sun spider for every failed
interview. All the same desert color as the walls of every apartment I've ever lived
in. The bones are buried deeper than I thought; I haven't hit anything yet. There's
dirt in my eyes, though, and the sweat from my brow is dripping down to my
eyelashes and when I blink, they mix and create a thin layer of mud over my pupils.
My hands are dry and cracked and I wonder how long it will take for my flesh to to

melt and rot and seep down into the cracks of the earth.

I pause to catch my breath; this is the hardest I've ever worked for something. My hands lie flat on the ground as I lean forward and let sweat fall in droplets and darken the sand. It's vibrating; the bones are getting closer, dancing in sync like my sister's freckles and my dry tongue behind my teeth. Bending down until my lips and forehead hit the sand too, I whisper to the bones and try to sooth them. I can tell they're restless and wanting to finally meet me. I think I hear them whispering back. This is how I pray. My gods are my bone friends and cousins and distant godfathers who can give my sister everything I haven't been able to.

It's difficult to breathe, there's a hitch in my throat as I try inhaling to alleviate the pressure in my lungs. Gritty flakes of earth scratch my teeth and throat and tongue but I force myself to keep digging anyway – to blindly dig as the mud and tears flow freely and frantically from my eyes. Inhale, dig, exhale, dig. There's a cramp in my abdomen. Everything is too hot.

When my sister and I were younger, thirteen or so, we were prohibited from speaking to each other and eating carbs. Not because of our parents or our teachers – we just started worshipping the same glossy monthly magazines at the same time. Sisters by blood and by starvation, we spaced our days perfectly between meals. The way the pizza crust tasted after five days of only water and saltines was loud enough to substitute for conversation, and we moaned into it. We ate entire boxes in one sitting, we drank the red sauce and let the melting cheese tie its way around our arteries and asses.

Showing skin was forbidden until we met our goal so, when we were alone, we took off our clothes and looked at where the pockets of fat sat low on our hips. We vowed to follow the rules next time and not eat so much pizza. We slapped at the new stretch marks on our upper thighs, felt our palms vibrating in our bones. There was a wardrobe full of bright pink sweatsuits and we stuffed ourselves into them to hide our curves.

When we stepped out into the world, into the ossuary that was reality, and stood in the donation line to give our bodies up to a greater cause – to jobs and boyfriends and social lives, we looked out of place. I felt right at home, walking amongst all those who were dead around me, standing upright and shuffling onto the subway and into the office and into stiff beds. And my sister looked at me with curious eyes, searching for our old tribes and past lives in my protruding ribcage and bumpy spine.

She suddenly became the scientist studying my body, she started healing and eating and coping while I continued to rot, my stomach sinking farther into my bones. The glint in her eyes was bright—intrigued and fearful—as my bone colosseum continued to rise in front of her. I was spread out on an examination table and she thrived, she studied, she stood tall. She learned words. She ate pizza. She became interesting and important and needed in her field of study. I was useful to her. My purpose was to help her fulfill hers, despite her worried hands always pushing the plate toward me.

Now it's her job to study the bones of the dead and I'm not useful to her like this. I need to die in a more physical way. I think about what she said, about her life's purpose being to find the purpose of other lives. Why couldn't I do that, too? I've tried many times, to sacrifice myself to her so she could study more, so she could be with me all day. But I always backed out just in time.

The kids in the neighborhood would call me a bitch if I used anything other than my fists. When I was growing up, everyone settled everything with hands only, so if you caught me with a gun it's only because I was taking yours from you and tucking it safely in the dumpster.

It stuck with me, and that day, one hot day my sophomore year of college, I really felt like using my fists. I took a walk and a cop asked me where I was going, how I was doing today, wasn't the weather nice. I couldn't punch him but I balled my hand in a fist and let my fingernails tell my palm what was up.

I'm going to my friend's house, I'm doing okay, we have to study for a test, yes I love when it's sunny but I don't think I'll get to enjoy it much today since I'll be studying.

He patted his fat gut and smiled. Stay in school, study hard, I wish I did.

Yes, I wish you did too. If you had gotten another job I'd be able to punch you, and the blood pooling just on the surface of my skin, where bruises the shape of my fingernails are forming, would burst all over your suit or lab coat or collared Verizon Wireless shirt. He asked what I was majoring in and I thought, right then, I loved a man in uniform, and maybe he would be the perfect one to kill me. And maybe, since he was handsome, I could punch him and let him shoot me and I would be okay with him getting away with murder because at least he was sexy.

Instead I smiled and was nice because I was weak. He walked away and I cradled my fist in my hand all the way home and washed it in the sink, polished it with Neosporin and rubbing alcohol. I wrapped it in satin and put in on the top shelf behind the the old scrapbooks and shoeboxes and saved it for later. I wondered if I'd ever be able to use my hands to get what I wanted.

I'm still not sure about the logistics of burying oneself alive. Even now, as I finally dig deep enough and see dusty skeletons peeking at me. I've done enough, I've found someone to keep me company. Someone I can learn from. When they find me, days from now probably, my sister and my mother and the cops, I'll already be suffocated and smelly and my flesh will probably be tender enough to rip from the bone easily. I hope my sister's eyes sparkle. And she won't even remember that she hasn't returned my calls in a month, or seen me in two. As soon as she digs me up again, she'll remember who I am and she'll love me for my sacrifice, just like I loved her for hers.

I crouch into the hole, taking a handful of earth from the surface with me, watching as streams of it escape from between my fingers. As it falls dryly on my leg, the puffs of dirt that rise in the aftermath taste nothing like cinnamon—nothing like the pan of cinnamon buns I binge eat after work on Fridays. I feel the bones underfoot trying to poke their way through the soles of my boots, the callouses on the heels of my feet rub themselves into my sweaty socks in search of moisture. My toes chafe. The brown sugar, it's settling on my tongue and in my grimy eyes. I blink once and the world is brown, twice and it's technicolor, my pupils blown wide into stain glass goggles. I feel scorpions in my mouth—or dragonflies: wings flapping, traumatized as they fall down my throat and find a stomach-cave too small and too empty to settle in. I lift myself to the edge of the hole and pull as much of that powder in as I can with my tired excavator arms. I hug it close to my body and fall back in, back on my knees. The bones clatter. They are reforming under and around me, ossein crop circles hidden under feet of tightly packed moon sand, trying to find a way to glow dully in the desert. A welcome party for me. The bass of the music assists me in covering myself. The grains move in waves, vibrating against each other, making hushed noises as they crash together in the crescendo of the desert synth humming underground. The sand is at my neck now. Then my mouth. I'm almost covered, and I chew on the the muddy Friday-night-cinnamon-roll mess until I my throat is swollen shut. A comforting bone finger curls around my pinky, telling me it's okay, tugging me deeper. It feels like my sister. My eyes water and I try looking up at the sky before I blink again and it goes black.

Scan the QR code above to visit the Tumblr for Glyph 2018, where there will be updates and art from SFUAD alumni.

Scan the QR code below to view the Glyph 2018 art eBook.

www.ingramcontent.com/pod-product-compliance
Lightning Source LLC
Chambersburg PA
CBHW030007190526
45157CB00014B/895